おとなのORIGAMI-BOOK

cochaeの
グラフィック折り紙

妖怪おりがみ

YŌKAI ORIGAMI

Bilingual, in Japanese and English

講談社

はじめに Introduction

　私たちが、日本の伝統的な遊び「折り紙」に絵柄をつけたものを「グラフィック折り紙」として作り始めたのは、2003年のことでした。折る前の状態でも、折っていくプロセスでも、色や柄の重なり、幾何学模様を楽しめるように作っています。折ったあとはオブジェとして飾ることができ、見て、触って、飾って、とさまざまな楽しみ方ができる折り紙なのです。
　折り紙の技法が親から子に伝承されることが少なくなってきたのと同様に、妖怪の話を親から子に語り伝えることも少なくなってきました。昔は家の中で一緒に暮らしていた（？）不気味だけど愛らしい妖怪たちも、今では影を潜めています。折り紙と妖怪。この日本独自の伝承文化を合わせてみよう、と考えてこの本を作りました。愛らしくて楽しい妖怪たちを選び、シンプルな形に仕上がるようにグラフィックを工夫してみました。
　折り紙を折りながら、妖怪に思いを馳せ、折った妖怪を生活空間の中に飾ってみて下さい。意外とすぐ近くに、妖怪の存在を嗅ぎとることができるかもしれません。この本が、折り紙と妖怪を楽しく思い出すきっかけになれば幸いです。

こちゃえ
cochae

目次 Contents

はじめに | 4
Introduction

妖怪おりがみ ラインナップ | 6
YŌKAI Origami Line up

日本の妖怪のこと | 12
What Are Yōkai?

妖怪日本地図 | 14
YŌKAI map

基本の折り図記号 | 16
Basic Origami Folds

24枚の妖怪おりがみ 解説付き | 17
"24 YŌKAI Origami with Explanation"

折り図 | 65
Instructions & Diagrams

この本の使い方
How to use this book.

● ミシン目で折り紙をカットし、
p65からの折り図を見ながら折ってみましょう。
Let's fold the paper using the pictures and diagrams from p65 after cutting the paper along the machine line.

● ☆マークは、難易度のレベルを表しています。
Star express the degree of difficulty.

> ★　　簡単！ is easy
> ★★　やや簡単 is intermediate
> ★★★ ちょっと難しい is more difficult

●「折り図記号」や、複数の折り方に共通する
「基本の折り方」は、p16を参照してください。
See p16, for an explanation of folding symbols and basic folding.

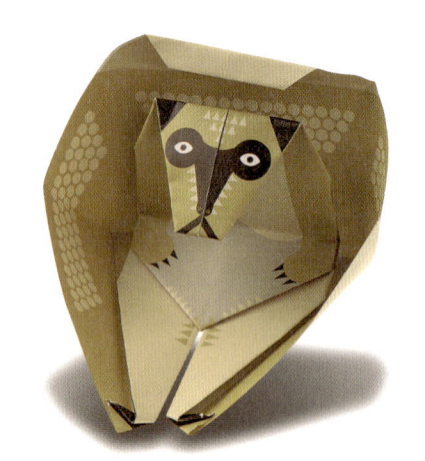

ふたくちおんな
二口女 ★★
Futakuchi-Onna

17

まめだぬき
豆狸 ★★
Mame-Danuki

19

おとろし ★
Otoroshi

21

がごぜ
元興寺 ★★
Gagoze

23

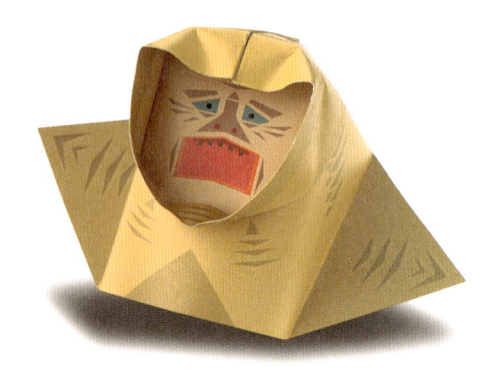

しろうかり
白うかり ★
Shiro-Ukari

25

あかくち
赤口 ★
Akakuchi

27

ぬっぺっぽう ★★
Nuppeppō

29

ひとつめこぞう
一つ目小僧 ★
Hitotsume-Kozō

31

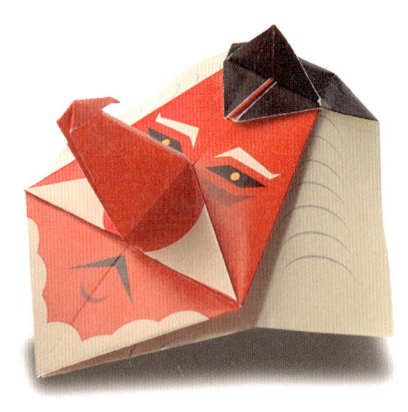

てんぐ
天狗 ★★
Tengu

33

ぶらぶら
不落不落 ★★
Bura-Bura

35

いぬがみ
犬神 ★
Inugami

37

にんぎょ
人魚 ★★
Ningyo

39

ごたいめん
五体面 ★★
Gotaimen

+1

うぶめ
産女 ★
Ubume

+3

てのめ
手の目 ★★
Te-no-Me

+5

あめふりこぞう
雨降り小僧 ★★
Amefuri-Kozō

+7

あかなめ
垢嘗め ★★
Aka-Name

49

あみきり
網切り ★★
Ami-Kiri

51

ぬれおんな
ぬれ女 ★★
Nure-Onna

53

にほんあし
二本足 ★★★
Nihon-Ashi

55

ろくろくび
ろくろ首 ★★★
Rokuro-Kubi

—— 57 ——

あずきあらい
小豆洗い ★★★
Azuki-Arai

—— 59 ——

かっぱ
河童 ★★★
Kappa

—— 61 ——

てんじょうくだり
天井下り ★★★
Tenjō-Kudari

—— 63 ——

日本の妖怪のこと

　日本には、妖怪にまつわる逸話や伝説が多く残っています。たとえば、平安時代初期に成立した日本最古の説話集『日本霊異記』には、奈良の元興寺に現れた鬼が童子をとり殺す話があり、また平安時代後期の歴史物語『大鏡』には、とある右大臣が百鬼夜行と遭遇する話があります。

　百鬼夜行というのは、多種多様な化け物の群れがにぎやかに行進するもので、これに出くわしたら、じっと固唾をのんで通り過ぎるのを待つしかないといいます。とくに人間に危害を加えることはないようですが……。

　ところで、妖怪（オバケ）と幽霊とはどうちがうのでしょうか？　これについては、民俗学者の柳田國男が『妖怪談義』のなかで定義しています。

1、妖怪は出現する場所がたいていは定まっている。これに反して幽霊の方は、てくてくと向うからやって来るもので、これに狙われたら、どれほど遠くへ逃げていても追いかけられる。

2、妖怪は相手を選ばず、多数に向かって交渉しようとしているように見える。対して幽霊は、これぞと思う者だけに思い知らせようとする。

3、妖怪は宵と暁の薄明かりの時刻に登場することが多い。幽霊は草木も眠る暗闇の中に現れる。

　日本人は、人工物である器なども99年経てば「つくも神」という妖怪になると考え、また、どこからともなく小豆を洗うような音が聞こえれば「小豆洗い」という名の妖怪がいると信じました。長い歴史のなかで、人知では計り知れない現象として、妖怪たちに畏怖の念を抱いてきたのです。

　本書で紹介する妖怪は、江戸時代中・後期に、鳥山石燕や竹原春泉が描いた妖怪の画図や、熊本県八代の松井家に伝わる『百鬼夜行絵巻』などに描かれた図像を参考にしました。日本の伝統的な妖怪たちとの出会いを楽しんでください。

What Are Yōkai?

Japan has many legends and anecdotes about the supernatural beings known collectively as *yōkai*. A story in the *Nihon ryōiki* (An Account of Miracles in Japan), which was compiled in the early Heian period (around 822), describes a demon at Nara's Gangōji temple that kills children. In the late-Heian historical text *Ōkagami* (The Great Mirror), the Minister of the Right encounters a motley bunch of demons making their way noisily through the streets one night. If you ever encounter one of these spooky but not particularly menacing parades, you'd better just hold your breath and wait for it to pass.

Incidentally, *yōkai* are not the same as ghosts (*yūrei*). The folklore scholar Kunio Yanagita (1875–1962) defined the difference:

1) *Yōkai* always appear in a particular place. Ghosts, on the other hand, approach you—and will pursue you to the ends of the earth.
2) *Yōkai* are not generally fussy about who they have contact with, while ghosts pick on a particular person they want to teach a lesson.
3) Whereas *yōkai* often inhabit the half-light of early evening and daybreak, ghosts appear in the dead of night when the world is asleep.

The Japanese used to believe that a manmade container will, after ninety-nine years, turn into a *Tsukumo-Gami*, and that the sound of azuki beans being washed means an *Azuki-Arai* is nearby. As unfathomable as ever, the *yōkai* are still held in awe.

The illustrations for the *yōkai* origami in this book are based on prints by the Edo-period *ukiyo-e* artists Toriyama Sekien and Takehara Shunsen, as well as the *Hyakki yagyō emaki* (*Hyakki Yagyō* Picture Scrolls) in the archives of the Matsui family in Kumamoto Prefecture in Kyūshū. We hope you have fun meeting these traditional Japanese spooks!

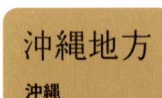

妖怪日本地図

日本全国津々浦々、神代(かみよ)のころより妖怪は各地に現れ、伝承として、あるいは絵画として残されています。
妖怪は定住するタイプがほとんどですが、天狗や河童のように移動するものもいます。
ここでは、この本で紹介する妖怪と、そのほかの代表的な妖怪が暮らすおもな場所を都道府県別に表してみました。
夜、灯りを消して、暗がりのなかで耳をすませてみてください。妖怪たちのおしゃべりが聞こえてくるかもしれません。

中国地方

鳥取
小豆洗い
島根
ぬれ女
岡山
豆狸／一つ目小僧／砂かけ婆
広島
海坊主
山口
産女

近畿地方

三重
磯天狗
滋賀
人魚／天狗
京都
天狗／手の目／不落不落／鬼／酒呑童子
奈良
元興寺／天狗／鬼／砂かけ婆
和歌山
鬼／烏天狗
大阪
豆狸
兵庫
豆狸／砂かけ婆

九州地方

福岡
産女／人魚／ぬれ女／ぬりかべ
佐賀
あやかし
長崎
ぬれ女／産女
大分
産女／海坊主
熊本
ろくろ首／河童
宮崎
産女／一反木綿／鬼火／火車
鹿児島
一反木綿／人面魚

沖縄地方

沖縄
人魚／犬神

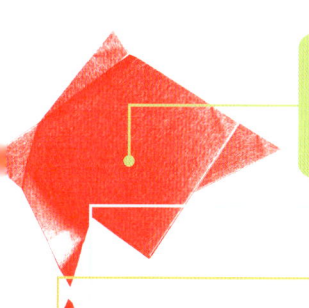

北海道地方

北海道
河童／一つ目お化け

東北地方

青森
雪女
岩手
座敷童子／雪女
秋田
座敷童子
宮城
海坊主／提灯小僧
山形
山姥
福島

関東地方

栃木
天狗／砂まき狸
茨城
天狗／河童／二口女
群馬
分福茶釜
千葉
二口女／だいだらぼっち／あやかし
埼玉
袖引き小僧／小豆婆
東京
小豆洗い／一つ目小僧／河童／おいてけ堀
神奈川
一つ目小僧／天狗

北陸・甲信越・中部地方

富山
人魚／雪男／雪入道
石川
海鳴り子坊主
福井
人魚／首なし馬
新潟
ろくろ首／ぬれ女／鎌いたち
長野
小豆洗い／一つ目小僧
山梨
小豆洗い／一つ目小僧
静岡
天狗／ろくろ首／一つ目小僧／洗濯狐
愛知
一つ目小僧／海坊主／入道坊主
岐阜
天狗／雪入道／鎌いたち

四国地方

香川
犬神／ろくろ首／天狗／鬼
徳島
小豆洗い／犬神／天狗／豆狸／子泣き爺／山姥
愛媛
産女／犬神／ろくろ首
高知
小豆洗い

注
※白文字が本書で紹介する妖怪、黒文字がそれ以外のおもな妖怪です。
なお、赤口、ぬっぺっぽう、白うかり、五体面、雨降り小僧、垢嘗め、二本足、天井下りの棲息地は不明です。

基本的な折り図記号を覚えよう
Basic Origami Folds

折り紙を折る前に、折り図の記号を覚えましょう。
これさえ覚えれば、折り図（p65〜）が簡単にわかります。

Before starting on your origami, familiarizing yourself with these basic folds will make it easier to follow the instructions (which begin on page 65).

移動線 Direction line

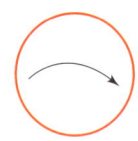

紙の移動を表します。矢印の始点と終点をよく見て、どのように移動しているかを確認しましょう。

Look carefully at the starting and end points of the arrow: it will show you the direction the paper needs to be folded.

谷折り Valley fold

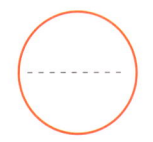

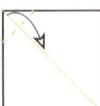

山折り Mountain fold

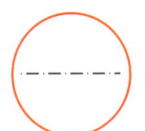

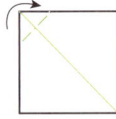

折り線をつける Make a crease

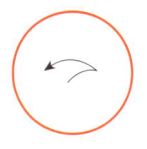

1つの図で表しますが、実際には2工程あります。

There is just one crease in the diagram shown here, but sometimes there are as many as three.

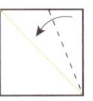

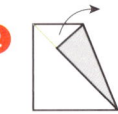

中割り折り Inside reverse fold

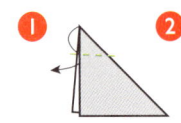

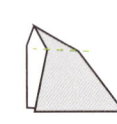

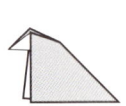

鶴の頭の折り方も、中割り折りですね。
An inside reverse fold is used on the crane's head, too.

かぶせ折り Outside reverse fold

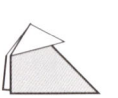

段折り Stair fold

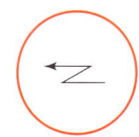

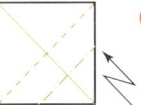

16

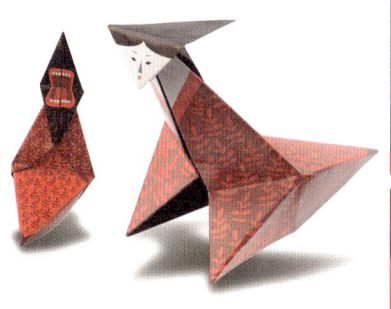

二口女
Futakuchi-Onna
ふたくちおんな
★★

後頭部にも口のある、女の妖怪。蛇のような髪の毛が、うしろの口に食べものを運び、箸の代わりをします。継子を憎み、食べものを与えず餓死させると、報いとして二口女になるともいわれています。

A woman with an extra mouth on the back of her head that is fed by the serpent-like tendrils of her hair. Women are said to become a *Futakuchi-Onna* as punishment for starving a stepchild to death.

17　→ 折り図 p65

ふたくちおんな
二口女
Futakuchi-Onna

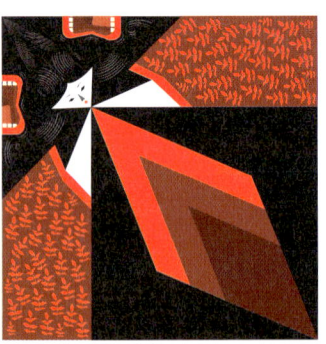

竹原春泉画

豆狸
Mame-Danuki

睾丸に息を吹きかけると8畳くらいに広がり、それをかぶって異形の姿に変身するというトンデモ妖怪。雨の降る夜、陰嚢を笠にして出かけることも。おもに西日本の旧家に棲息しています。

A somewhat comical raccoon-dog that transforms its appearance by blowing into its testicles to stretch them up to room size, and using them as an umbrella on rainy nights. *Mame-Danuki* mainly inhabit old houses in western Japan.

→ 折り図 p66

豆狸
Mame-Danuki

竹原春泉画

おとろし
Otoroshi

寺や神社に棲む、毛むくじゃらの妖怪。不信心な人が寺や神社に入ろうとすると、突然屋根から落ちておどかします。「おどろおどろしい」という言葉が「おとろし」という名前になったようです。

A hairy beast living in temples and shrines that suddenly drops down from the roof to menace any impious person who chances by. Its name derives from the word *odoro-odoroshii*, meaning "hair-raising."

→ 折り図 p68

おとろし
Otoroshi

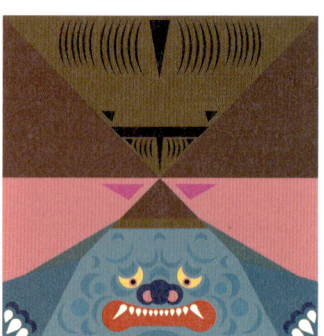

鳥山石燕画

元興寺
Gagoze

★★

日本の妖怪の元祖。飛鳥時代、奈良の元興寺の鐘楼に現れて人を食べた、鬼の一種です。西日本を中心に妖怪やお化けを「ガゴゼ」「ガゴジ」と呼ぶのは、この妖怪に由来するともいわれます。

Dating back to the sixth century, this demon that ate people passing by Nara's Gangōji temple bell is Japan's original *yōkai*. Monsters or other supernatural beings are often referred to as *gagoze* or *gagoji* in western Japan.

→ 折り図 p69

元興寺
Gagoze

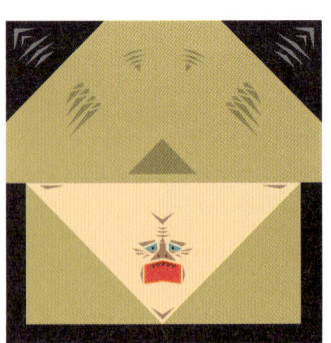

鳥山石燕画

白うかり
Shiro-Ukari

全身真っ白で、オットセイのようにつるんとした顔とヒゲ、大きく飛び出した目が特徴の妖怪。ぼんやり、ふわふわと風にたなびき、漂っている癒し系の妖怪です。

This all-white creature resembles a seal with its silky face and whiskers, and large bulging eyes. A light wisp drifting dreamily in the breeze, it is associated with healing.

→ 折り図 p70

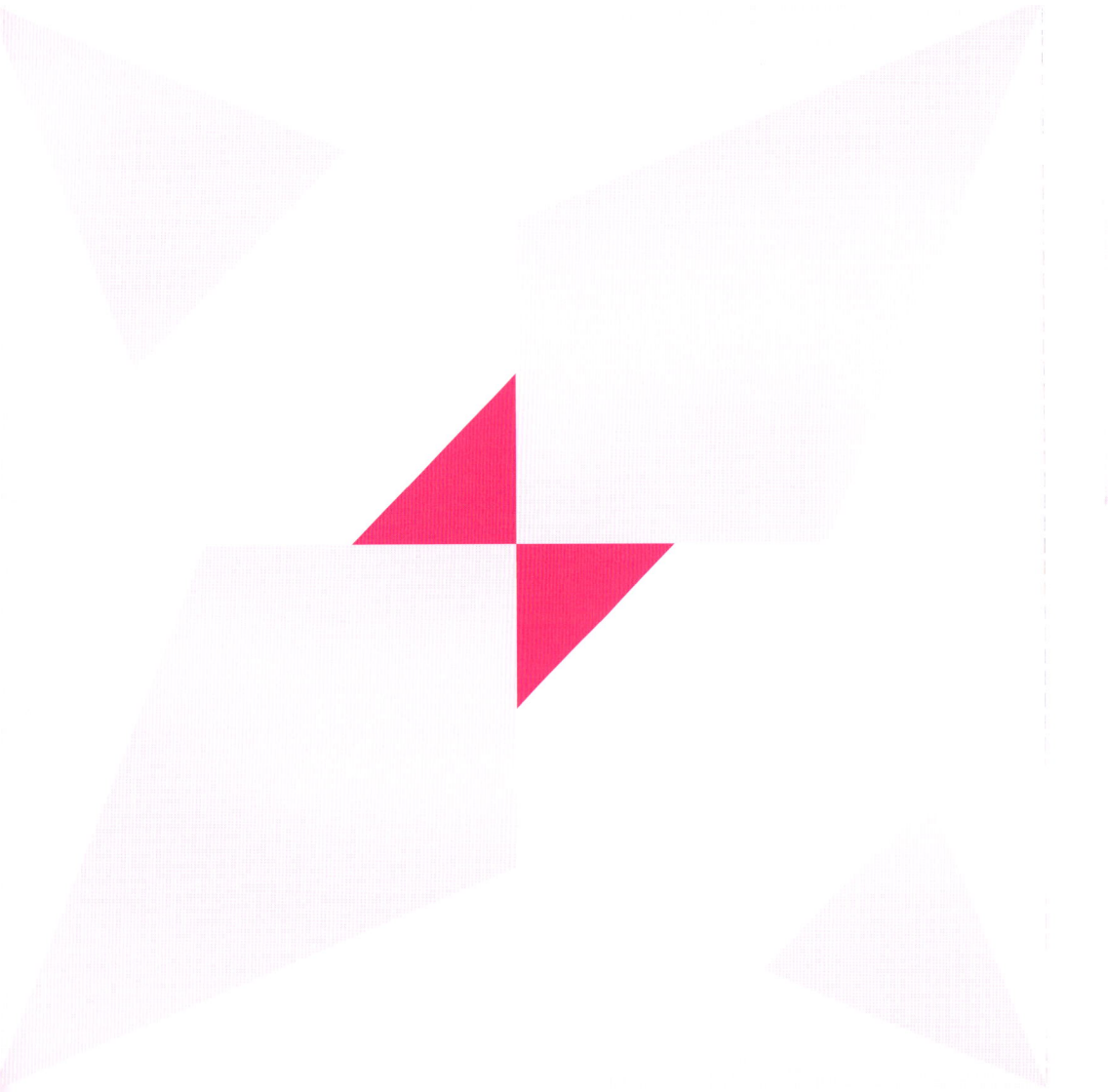

白うかり
しろうかり
Shiro-Ukari

松井文庫「百鬼夜行絵巻」

赤口
あかくち
Akakuchi

大きな口から赤い舌を出す妖怪。赤口とは、もともと陰陽道の凶日のこと。血や炎をイメージさせる不気味な赤口の日のイメージが、この妖怪を生みました。

A monster with bright red bristling hair and red tongue protruding from its large mouth. It is named after the unlucky *shakku no hi*, or "red-mouth day," portentous of blood or flames.

→ 折り図 p72

あかくち
赤口
Akakuchi

鳥山石燕画

ぬっぺっぽう
Nuppeppō

★★

「のっぺらぼう」の仲間で、腹部に目鼻のようなシワがある妖怪です。廃寺や墓地に棲み、夜になると、あてもなく散歩に出かけます。「ぬっぺふほふ」とも呼ばれます。

A companion of the faceless *Nopperabō*, this *yōkai* has wrinkles resembling a nose and eyes on its belly. It lives in ruined temples or graveyards, and wanders aimlessly at night.

→ 折り図 p73

ぬっぺっぽう
Nuppeppō

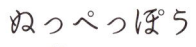

鳥山石燕画

一つ目小僧
Hitotsume-Kozō

一つ目の妖怪は多くいますが、小さな子どもの姿をしているのが一つ目小僧。いたずら好きで、山野や古い屋敷に現れては人間を驚かせ、舌をぺろりと出します。

The only small child among the numerous one-eyed *yōkai*, *Hitotsume-Kozō* likes nothing better than getting up to mischief. It appears in rural areas and old houses, sticking its tongue out to frighten humans.

→ 折り図 p74

一つ目小僧
ひとつめこぞう
Hitotsume-Kozō

鳥山石燕画
一つ目は坊主として
描かれることも多い。

天狗
てんぐ
Tengu ★★

全国の深山に棲む、日本の妖怪の代表。空を飛んだり、さまざまなものに変身したり、暴風を起こしたりと、強力な神通力を発揮します。ときには人間にだまされる間抜けな一面もあり、憎めない存在。

Japan's archetypal *yōkai*, the *Tengu* makes its home deep in the mountains. It has supernatural strength and can fly, assume a variety of forms, whip up a fierce wind, but is sometimes outwitted by humans.

→ 折り図 p75

天狗
てんぐ
Tengu

鳥山石燕画

不落不落
Bura-Bura

★★

提灯の妖怪。提灯がぱっくり割れて、そこが口になり舌を出します。目もついています。暗い夜道などでぼんやりとした灯が見えたら、不落不落かもしれません。

This paper-lantern spook splits open the paper to form a mouth through which it sticks out its tongue. If you see a faint light on a dark lane at night, it's probably a Bura-Bura.

→ 折り図 p76

不落不落
Bura-Bura

鳥山石燕画

犬神
いぬがみ
Inugami

ネズミくらいの小動物とも、手のひらにのるくらいの犬だともいわれます。おもに西日本の農村で、霊となって人間にとり憑きます。突発的にとり憑かれる場合と、代々家系に憑く場合があります。

A mouse-sized creature or palm-sized dog that takes spirit form to possess humans. Best known in farming communities in western Japan, it sometimes possesses individuals but has also been known to run in families.

→ 折り図 p77

犬神
Inugami

鳥山石燕画

人魚
にんぎょ
Ningyo ★★

各地の海に出没する妖怪。言葉は話さず静かに鳴き、体はいい匂いがします。日本では、人魚が網にかかっても海に返すのが昔からの漁師のしきたり。しかし人魚の肉は、不老長寿の薬ともいわれます。

This sea creature cannot speak, but it has a gentle voice and pleasant fragrance. It is traditionally freed from fishing nets, although its flesh is said to be a potion for longevity.

→ 折り図 p78

にんぎょ
人魚
Ningyo

鳥山石燕画

五体面
ごたいめん
Gotaimen
★★

大きな頭に手足がついた妖怪。百面相をして人を笑わせるのが好きな、お笑い系の妖怪です。自分の芸がうけず、笑ってもらえないときは暴れまわり、泣き、ふて寝をしてしまいます。

A big head with hands and feet that loves to make people laugh by pulling funny faces. If you fail to laugh, though, it throws a tantrum, bursts into tears, or sulks in bed.

→ 折り図 p80

五体面
Gotaimen

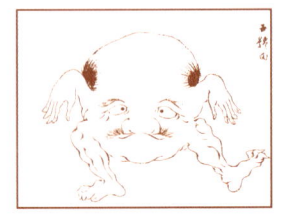

松井文庫「百鬼夜行絵巻」

産女
Ubume

<small>うぶめ</small>

通りかかる人に「子どもを抱いてください」とせがむ母親の妖怪。しかし、抱くと重くなって離れなくなってしまうので要注意。難産で亡くなった母親の霊が成仏できず、妖怪化したといわれます。

This mother pesters passers-by to hold her baby, but the unwary find they are unable to put it down although it is unbearably heavy. Apparently the restless spirit of a woman who died during childbirth.

→ 折り図 p81

産女
うぶめ
Ubume

鳥山石燕画

手の目
Te-no-Me

座頭姿で、手のひらに目がついた盲人の妖怪。人影のない草むらなどに出没します。強奪され殺された罪のない盲人の怨念が、この妖怪を生みました。

A blind masseur with an eye on the palm of each hand, commonly encountered in deserted grassy areas, the *Te-no-Me* is said to be the spirit of an innocent blind man robbed and beaten to death.

→ 折り図 p79

手の目
Te-no-Me

鳥山石燕画

雨降り小僧
あめふりこぞう
Amefuri-Kozō ★★

雨を降らせる神様「雨師」に仕えている、かわいい子どもの妖怪。破れ傘をさし、ひでりの地に雨を降らせてまわります。提灯をふると雨が降るといわれます。

This cute boy in the service of the rain god *Ushi* carries a torn umbrella and goes around drought-stricken areas bringing rain with a shake of his small paper lantern.

→ 折り図 p82

雨降り小僧
Amefuri-Kozō

鳥山石燕画

48

垢嘗め
あかなめ ★★
Aka-Name

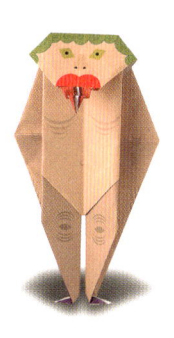

汚れた家や風呂屋に棲み、誰もいないときに現れては、長い舌で風呂場の垢をなめる妖怪。子どもの姿をしています。垢が積もって妖怪になりました。

A *yōkai* living in dirty houses or public baths that licks the grime off the bath with its long tongue. It grows out of the accumulated filth and takes the form of a child.

→ 折り図 p84

垢嘗め
あかなめ
Aka-Name

鳥山石燕画

50

網切り
あみきり
Ami-Kiri
★★

手が鋭いハサミになっていて、誰もいないときに、蚊帳や魚網や洗濯物をスッパリ切ってしまう妖怪。その切り口は、鋭い刃物で切り落としたかのよう。姿は海老やサソリに似ています。

A creature resembling a prawn or scorpion that appears when nobody is around to cut mosquito nets, fishing nets, and washing hung out to dry with its razor-sharp claws.

→ 折り図 p86

網切り
Ami-Kiri

鳥山石燕画

ぬれ女
Nure-Onna

海中から突然現れる妖怪。髪がいつもぬれており、体は大蛇。この妖怪はじつに凶暴で、殺人鬼。一度見つかったら、長い尻尾で必ず巻き取られ殺されてしまいます。

A woman with wet hair and the body of a large serpent that appears suddenly from the sea. A savage murderous demon, she kills anyone she chances upon by coiling them up in her tail.

→ 折り図 p87

ぬれ女
Nure-Onna

鳥山石燕画

二本足
にほんあし
Nihon-Ashi
★★★

胴体と手がなく、顔に足が二本ついている妖怪。はげ頭で血色がよい、愛敬のあるおじいさん。赤いふんどしをしめているのが特徴です。人に危害は加えません。

This *yōkai* has no body or hands, just two legs and a face. Bald, with a rosy complexion, it is an affable old man who typically wears a red loincloth and does not harm people.

→ 折り図 p88

二本足
Nihon-Ashi

松井文庫「百鬼夜行絵巻」

56

ろくろ首
Rokuro-Kubi
ろくろくび ★★★

全国で目撃されているメジャーな妖怪。女性が多く、細く首が伸びるタイプと、完全に首と胴体が分離するタイプがいます。寝ている間に首が伸びるので、妖怪だと自覚していない場合が多いようです。

A well-known *yōkai*, often female, that either stretches out its long neck or separates its head and neck from its body. Since it does this while asleep, it often fails to realize what it is doing.

→ 折り図 p90

ろくろ首
Rokuro-Kubi

鳥山石燕画

58

小豆洗い
あずきあらい
Azuki-Arai ★★★

ザクザクと小豆をとぐ音をさせて、人間を驚かせる妖怪。江戸では屋敷に出没したようですが、ふつうは川辺や橋の下などに出て、歌を歌うこともあります。近づくと、川に落とされるので注意。

A monster that frightens people with the sound of washing azuki beans. It commonly appears on riverbanks or under bridges, sometimes singing, and throws any unwary person who approaches it into the river.

→ 折り図 p91

小豆洗い
あずきあらい
Azuki-Arai

竹原春泉画

河童
かっば
Kappa ★★★

水に棲む妖怪で、あちらこちらで目撃されています。容姿は地方によって異なりますが、頭上に水をためる皿がついていて目が丸く、口がとがっているのが一般的。キュウリと相撲が大好き。

This water-dwelling creature is known throughout Japan. Its form varies according to the area, but it generally has a water-filled dish on its head, round eyes, and a pointed mouth. It loves cucumbers and *sumō* wrestling.

→ 折り図 p93

河童
Kappa

鳥山石燕画

天井下り
てんじょうくだり ★★★
Tenjō-Kudari

天井から逆さまにぶら下がっている妖怪。誰かを困らせたときに、この妖怪が天井から下りてくるとか。全身に毛が生えており、髪が長く、にやにや笑っています。

A *yōkai* that hangs upside down from the ceiling, only coming down in order to play pranks on people. It has a furry body, long hair, and a broad grin.

→ 折り図 p94

天井下り
Tenjō-Kudari

鳥山石燕画

★★ 二口女 Futakuchi-Onna → 折り紙 p17

折り図 Instructions & Diagrams

● 折り図の記号や、複数の折り方に共通する「基本の折り方」は、p16を参照してください。
See p16, for an explanation of folding symbols and basic folding.

1

2 裏返す
Turn over.

3

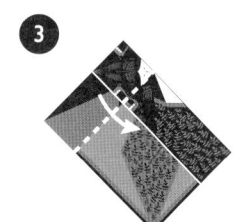

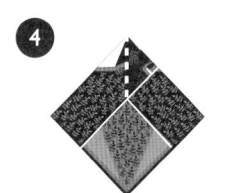

4 開いて顔を引っぱり出す
Unfold and pull out face.

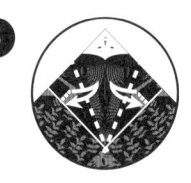

5 折り線を付ける
Make creases.

6 折り線を使って内側を広げてつぶすように折る
Open out and flatten along the creases.

7

8 折ったところ
The shape after step 7.

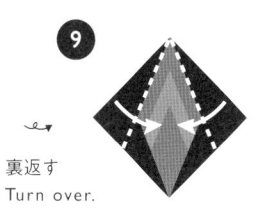

9 裏返す
Turn over.

10 上部を折り返して顔を見せる
Fold the top of the head back.

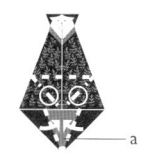

11 折り線をつけ、aを内側に折りながら○の部分をつまみあげるように折る
Fold flap <a> on both sides. Pinching the circles, pull up and fold over.

12 後ろへ少し山折りしておく
Fold back slightly using a mountain fold.

13 内側を開き、首を起こして形を整える
Pull open and raise head to finish off.

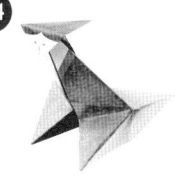

14 完成！
Finished!

豆狸 Mame-Danuki → 折り紙 p19

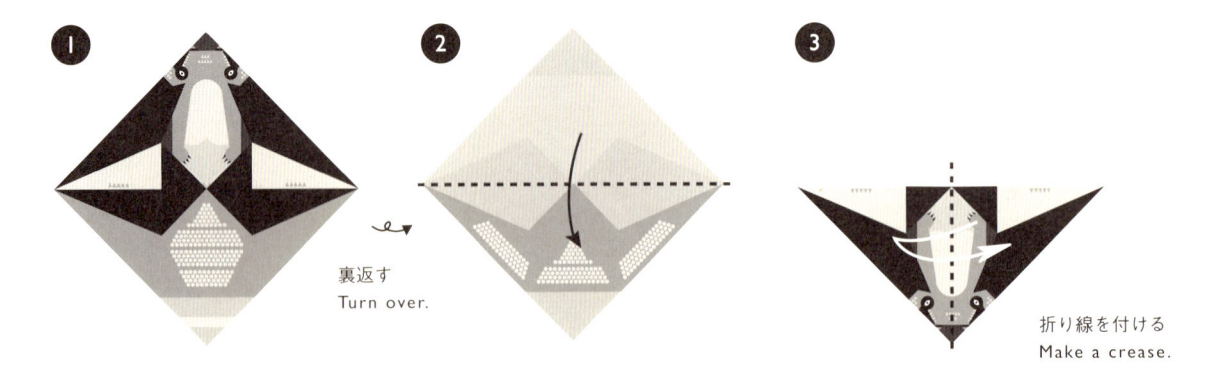

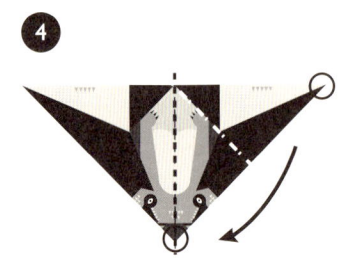

1

2 裏返す
Turn over.

3 折り線を付ける
Make a crease.

4 折り線を使って○と○を合わせるように開きながらつぶす
Open out along the crease and then fold over so the two circles meet.

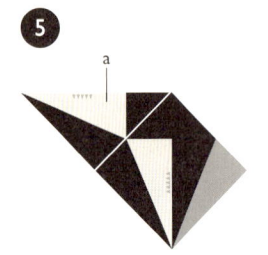

5 a側も3,4と同じように折る
Do the same to flap <a>.

6 折り線を付ける
Make creases.

7 折り線を使って内側を広げてつぶすように折る
Open out and flatten along the creases.

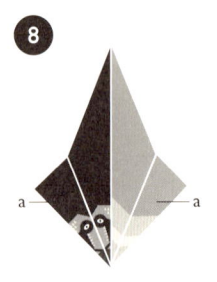

8 a側も6,7と同じように折る
Fold <a> as in steps 6 and 7.

9 裏返す
Turn over.

10 折り線を付ける
Make creases.

折り線を使って内側を広げて
つぶすように折る
Open out and flatten along
the creases.

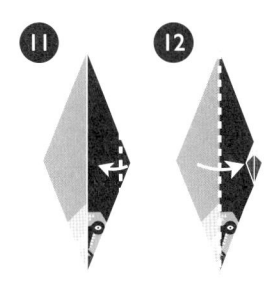

11 上の1枚のみ内側に折る
Fold the front flap on
the dotted line.

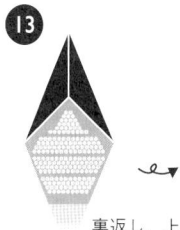

12

13 裏返し、上下の
向きを変える
Turn over, and
upside down.

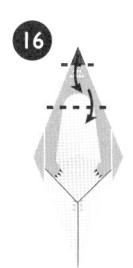

14

15

16 上の1枚を
2回谷折りして
顔を出す
Fold the front
flap twice.

17 後ろを広げて
内側に狸を座らせる
ように入れこむ
Open out the
back to reveal
the tanuki inside.

18 中割り折りで
足を作る
Make an inside
reverse fold for
the feet.

19 頭の上を
3回谷折り
Make three
valley folds.

20

21

22 少し上げる
Raise slightly.

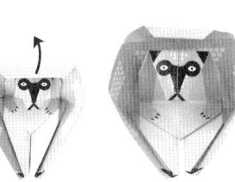

23 完成！
Finished!

おとろし Otoroshi → 折り紙 p21

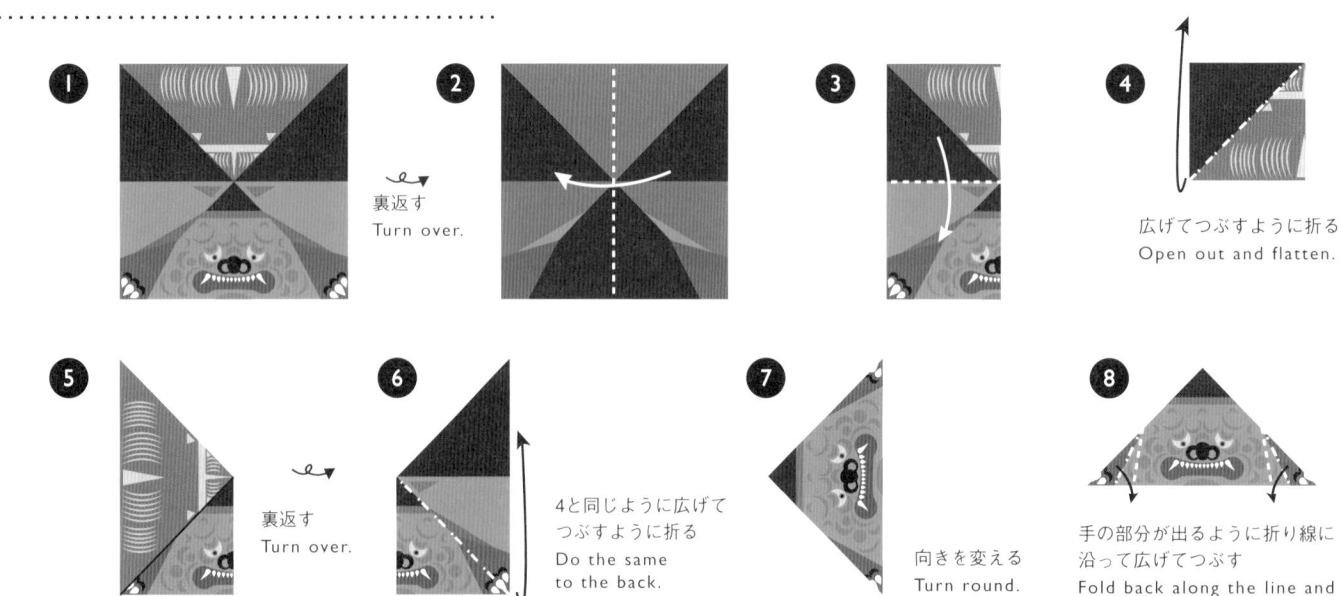

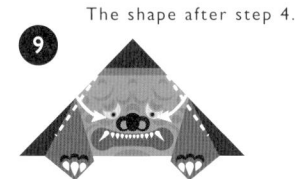

①

② 裏返す
Turn over.

③

④ 広げてつぶすように折る
Open out and flatten.

⑤ 裏返す
Turn over.
折ったところ
The shape after step 4.

⑥ 4と同じように広げて
つぶすように折る
Do the same to the back.

⑦ 向きを変える
Turn round.

⑧ 手の部分が出るように折り線に
沿って広げてつぶす
Fold back along the line and open up to show the paws.

⑨

⑩ 頭の上を2ヵ所谷折り
Make two valley folds.

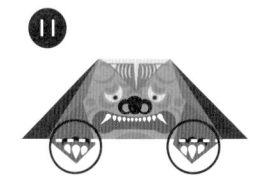

⑪ 手先を軽く谷折り
Make a slight valley fold.

⑫ 完成！
Finished!

68

元興寺 Gagoze → 折り紙 p23

1.

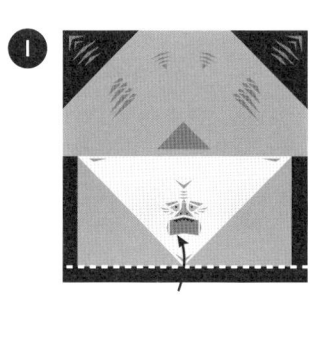

2.

3.
裏返す 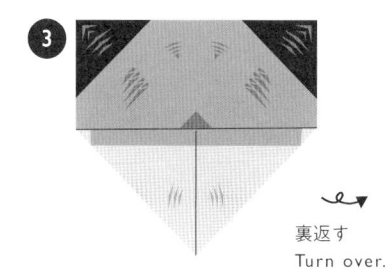
Turn over.

4.

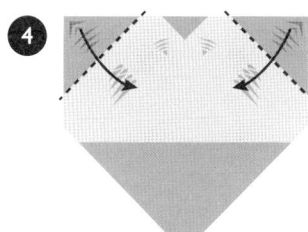

5.

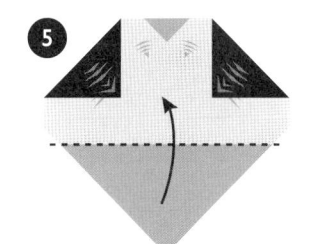

6.
折ったところ 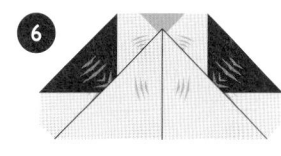
The shape after step 5.

7.
向きを変える
Turn round.

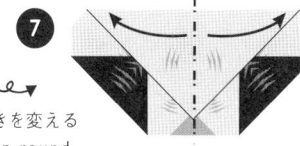

山折りし、丸みを付けながら円すい形に形造る
Fold up so that the circles meet to form a cone, keeping a round shape.

8. 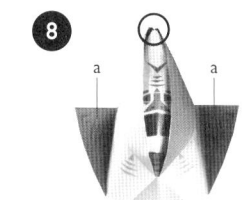
○の部分をつまみ、顔を押して平らにし、顔のまわりの部分に丸みをつける。aを広げる
Push down on the face and flatten then round out the paper circling the face.
Spread out flaps <a>.

9. 
完成！
Finished!

69

白うかり Shiro-Ukari → 折り紙 p25

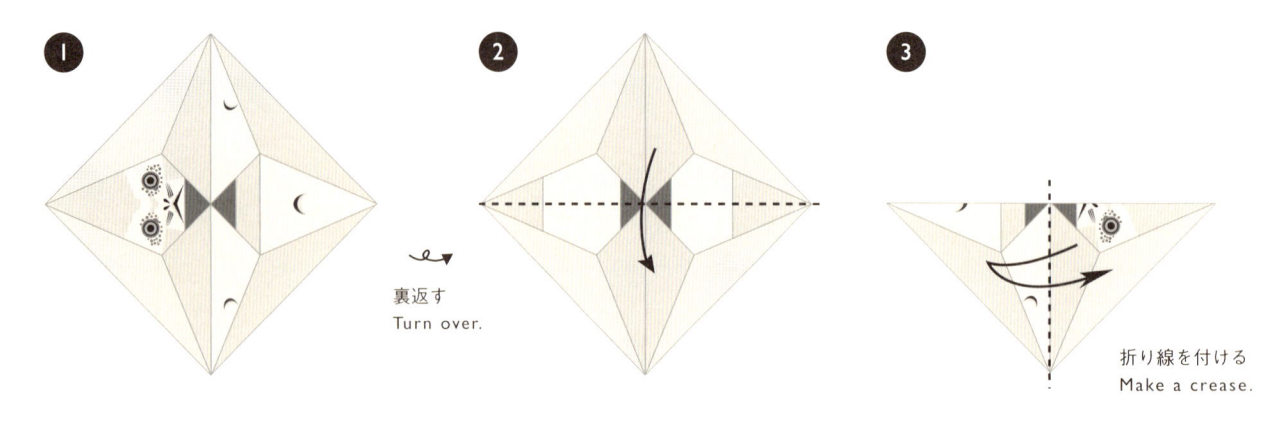

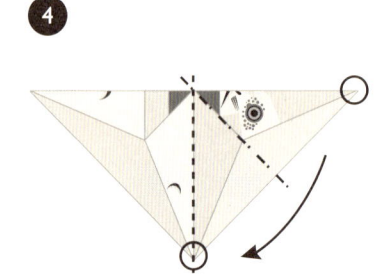

①

② 裏返す
Turn over.

③ 折り線を付ける
Make a crease.

④ 折り線を使って○と○を合わせるように開きながらつぶす
Open out along the crease and then fold over so the two circles meet.

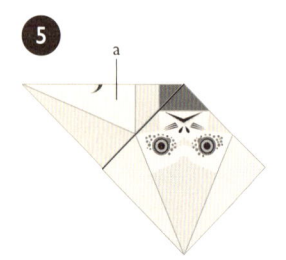

⑤ a 側も4と同じように折る
Do the same to the back.

⑥ 折り線を付ける
Make creases.

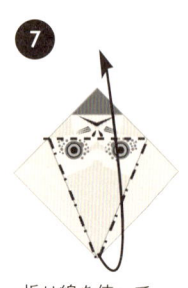

⑦ 折り線を使って内側を広げてつぶすように折る
Open out and flatten along the creases.

70

8

9
裏返す
Turn over.

10
折り線を付ける
Make creases.

11
折り線を使って内側を広げてつぶすように折る
Open out and flatten along the creases.

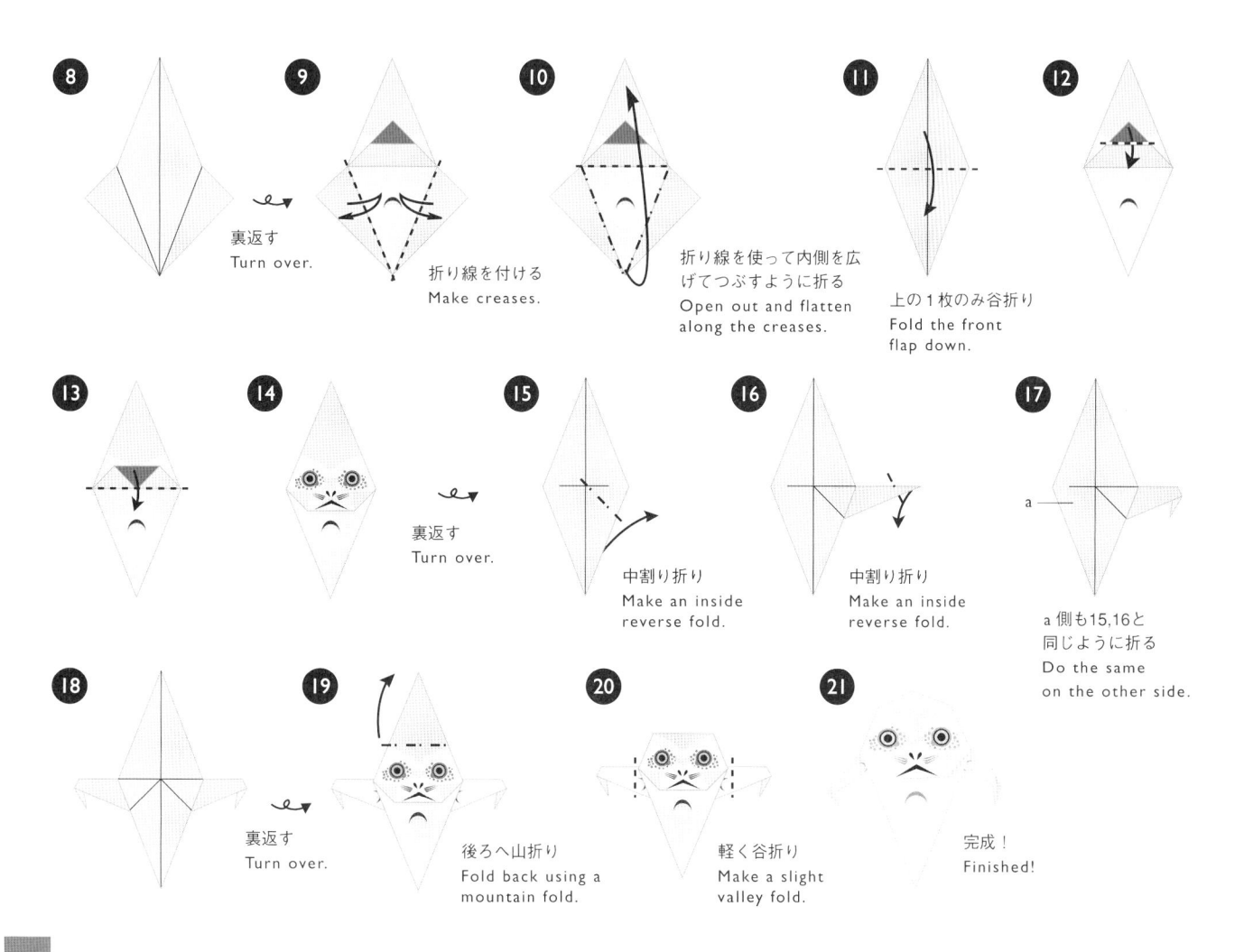

12
上の1枚のみ谷折り
Fold the front flap down.

13

14
裏返す
Turn over.

15
中割り折り
Make an inside reverse fold.

16
中割り折り
Make an inside reverse fold.

17
a側も15,16と同じように折る
Do the same on the other side.

18
裏返す
Turn over.

19
後ろへ山折り
Fold back using a mountain fold.

20
軽く谷折り
Make a slight valley fold.

21
完成！
Finished!

赤口 Akakuchi → 折り紙 p27

1

2 裏返す
Turn over.

3

4 白い部分を谷折り
Make a valley fold on the white section.

5

6

7 裏返し、向きを変える
Turn over and upside down.

8

9 折り線を付ける
Make creases.

10 折り線を使って鼻を作る
Fold along the creases to make the nose.

11 鼻を広げてつぶす
Open out the nose and flatten.

12 少し口を丸める
Pull up slightly to round out the mouth.

13 完成！
Finished!

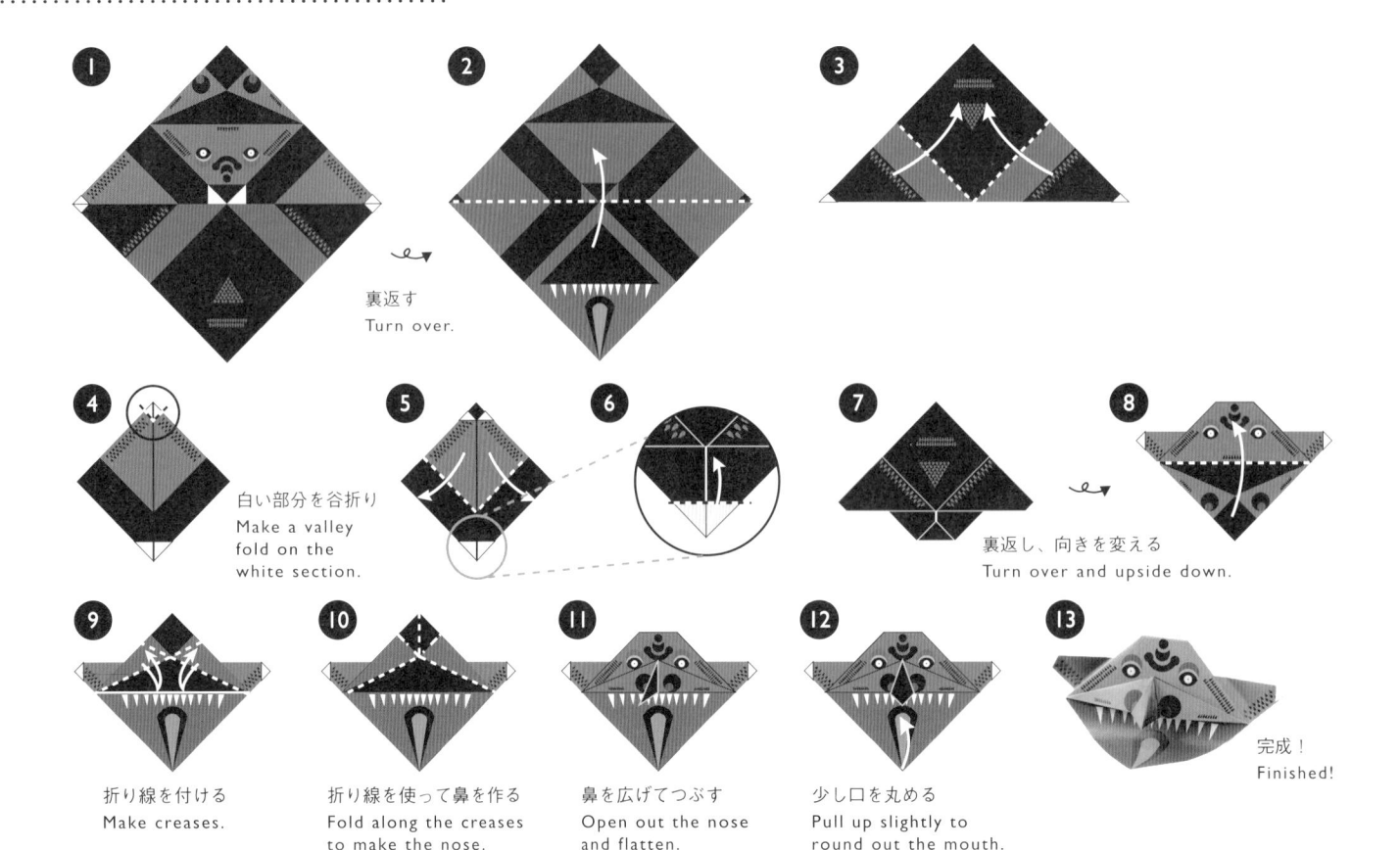

72

★★ ぬっぺっぽう Nuppeppō → 折り紙 p29

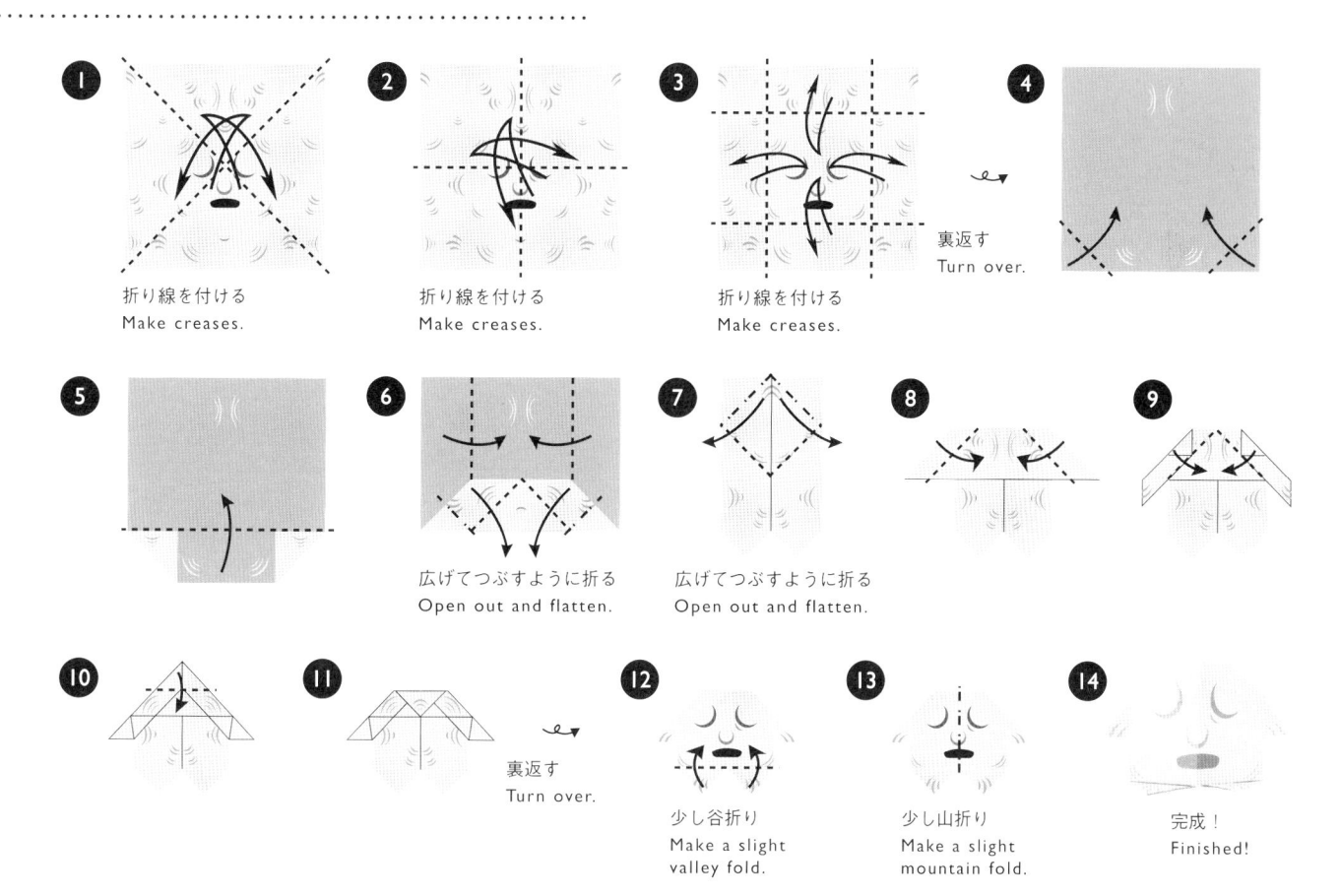

1 折り線を付ける
Make creases.

2 折り線を付ける
Make creases.

3 折り線を付ける
Make creases.

4 裏返す
Turn over.

5

6 広げてつぶすように折る
Open out and flatten.

7 広げてつぶすように折る
Open out and flatten.

8

9

10

11 裏返す
Turn over.

12 少し谷折り
Make a slight valley fold.

13 少し山折り
Make a slight mountain fold.

14 完成！
Finished!

★ 一つ目小僧 Hitotsume-Kozō → 折り紙 p31

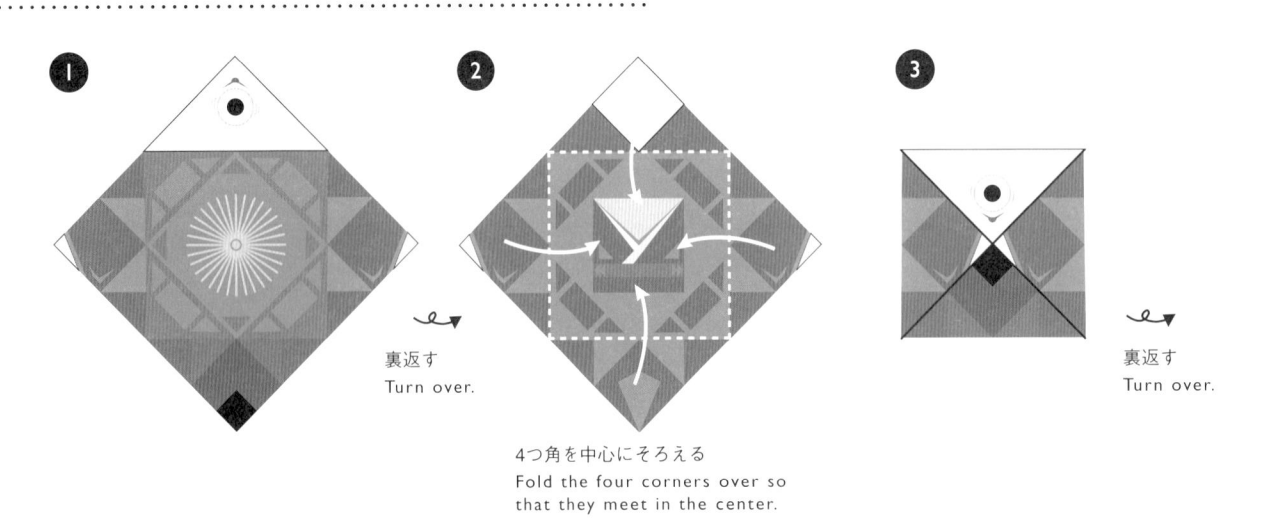

①

② 裏返す
Turn over.

4つ角を中心にそろえる
Fold the four corners over so that they meet in the center.

③ 裏返す
Turn over.

④ 4つ角を中心にそろえる
Fold the four corners over so that they meet in the center.

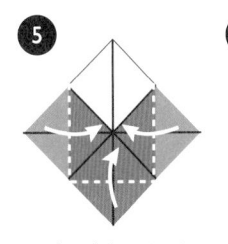

⑤ 3つ角を中心にそろえる
Fold three of the corners over to meet in the center.

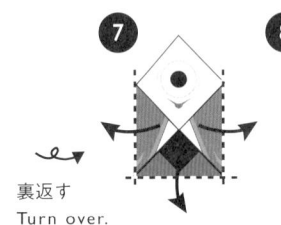

⑥ 裏返す
Turn over.

⑦ 少し広げる
Open out slightly.

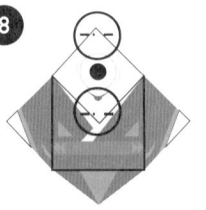

⑧ あごと頭を山折り
Make mountain folds on the head and chin.

⑨ 完成！
Finished!

天狗 Tengu → 折り紙 p33

1

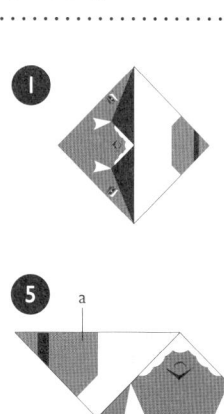

2 裏返す
Turn over.

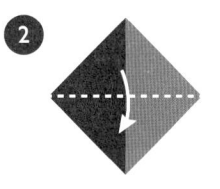

3 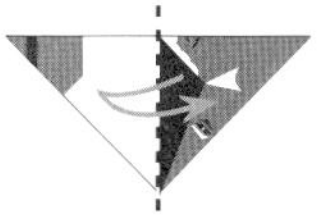 折り線を付ける
Make a crease.

4 折り線を使って○と○を合わせるように開きながらつぶす
Open out along the crease and then fold over so the two circles meet.

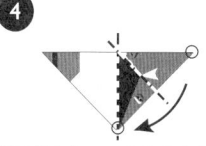

5 a側も4と同じように折る
Do the same to the back.

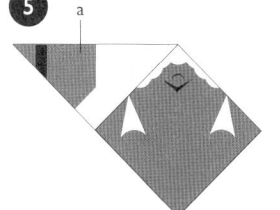

6 折り線を付ける
Make creases.

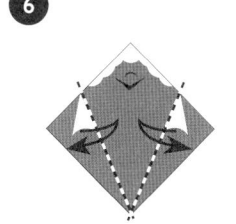

7 折り線を使って内側を広げてつぶすように折る
Open out and flatten along the creases.

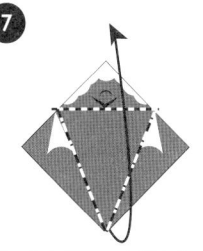

8 向きを変える
Turn upside down.
折り図記号に沿って鼻を立体にする
Pull out the nose as shown.

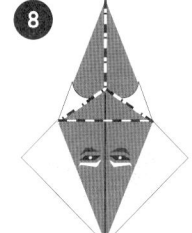

9 鼻先をかぶせ折り
Make an outside reverse fold on the nose.

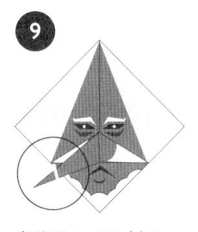

10

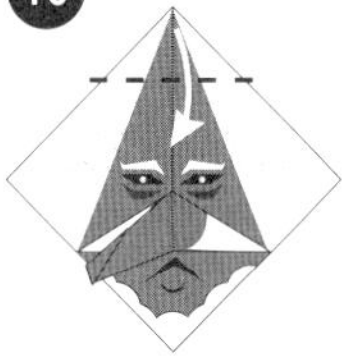

11 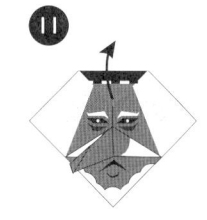 上の1枚を上へ
Fold the front flap up.

12 顔の脇を山折り
Make a slight mountain fold on each side of the face.

13 完成!
Finished!

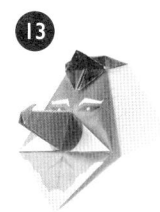

★★ 不落不落 Bura-Bura → 折り紙 p35

1.

2. 中心に合わせるように谷折り
Make valley folds to meet in the center.

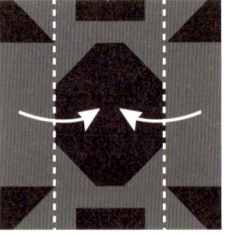

3.

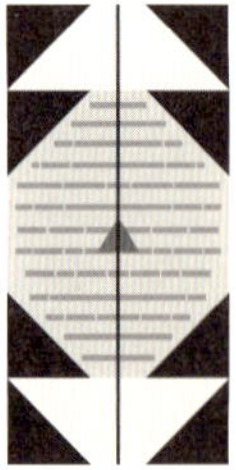

4. 裏返す
Turn over.

5.

6.

7. 裏返す
Turn over.

8.

9. 開きながらつぶす
Open out and flatten.

10. 表面の点線の部分をちぎる
Tear along the dotted line.

11. 軽く山折り
Make a slight mountain fold.

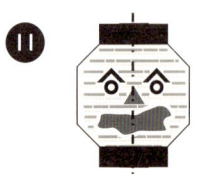

12. 完成！
Finished!

(step 1 → 裏返す Turn over.)
(step 3 → 裏返す Turn over.)

犬神 Inugami → 折り紙 p37

1

2 裏返す
Turn over.

3

4

5 上部を開いて顔を引っぱり出す
Unfold slightly and pull out the face.

6 折り線を付ける
Make creases.

7 折り線を使って内側を広げてつぶすように折る
Open out and flatten along the creases.

8 ←部分を少し谷折り
Make a slight valley fold by the arrow.

9

10

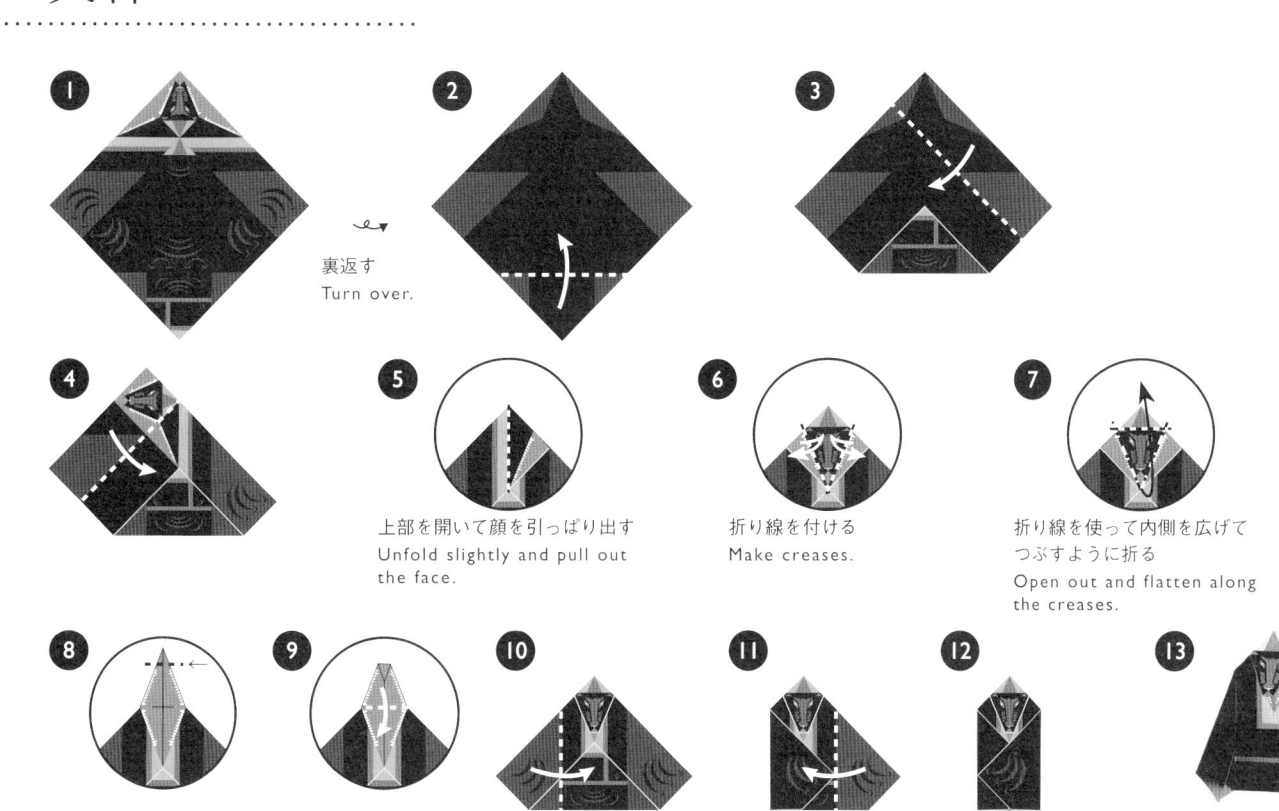

11

12 手を少し広げる
Open out the forelegs.

13 完成！
Finished!

★★ 人魚 Ningyo → 折り紙 p39

1

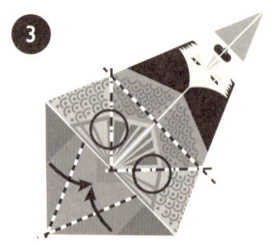

2 裏返す
Turn over.

3 ○の部分をつまみ上げるように折る
Pinching the circles, pull up and fold over.

4

5 山折り
Mountain fold.

6 半分に山折り
Fold in half making a mountain fold.

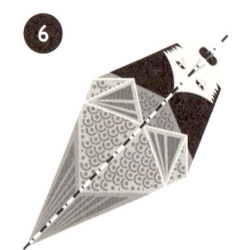

7 顔を開きながらつぶす
Unfold the face and flatten down.

8 顔の中心で山折り
Fold back using a mountain fold.

9 かぶせ折りで尾を上げる
Make an outside reverse fold to bring the tail up.

10 完成！
Finished!

★★ 手の目 Te-no-Me → 折り紙 p45

1.

2. 裏返す
Turn over.

3.

4.

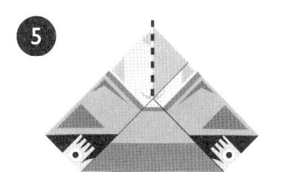

5. 上部を開いて顔を引っぱり出す
Unfold slightly and pull out face.

6. 裏面の色の境目の所に折り線を付ける
Make a crease along the borderline between colors on the back.

7. 折り線を使って内側を広げてつぶすように折る
Open out and flatten along the creases.

8. 折り線を付ける
Make creases.

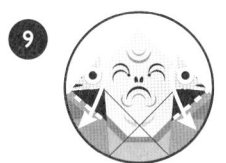

9. 折り線を使って内側を広げてつぶすように折る
Open out and flatten along the creases.

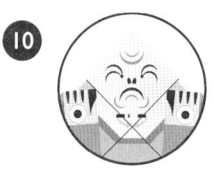

10. 顔の下を山折り
Make a mountain fold below the face.

11. 後ろへ山折りして手を広げ、形を整える
Fold back slightly using a mountain fold to finish off.

12. 完成！
Finished!

★★ 五体面 Gotaimen → 折り紙 p41

1

2 裏返す
Turn over.

3

4 広げてつぶすように折る
Open out and flatten.

5 裏返す
Turn over.

6 4と同じように広げてつぶすように折る
Do the same to the back.

7 後ろへ山折り
Fold back using a mountain fold.

裏返し、向きを変える
Turn over and then rotate.

8 開きながらつぶすように折る
Open out and flatten.

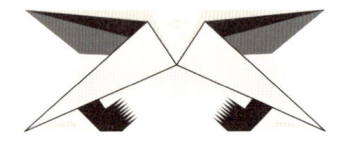

折ったところ
The shape after step 8.

80

9
10
11
12
13

裏返し、向きを変える
Turn over and then rotate.

14

足を谷折り
Make valley folds for the legs.

15

軽く谷折り。aをうしろで
つまみ、くぼみをつくる
Make slight valley folds.
Pinch the back of the face at point <a> to make a dent.

16

完成！
Finished!

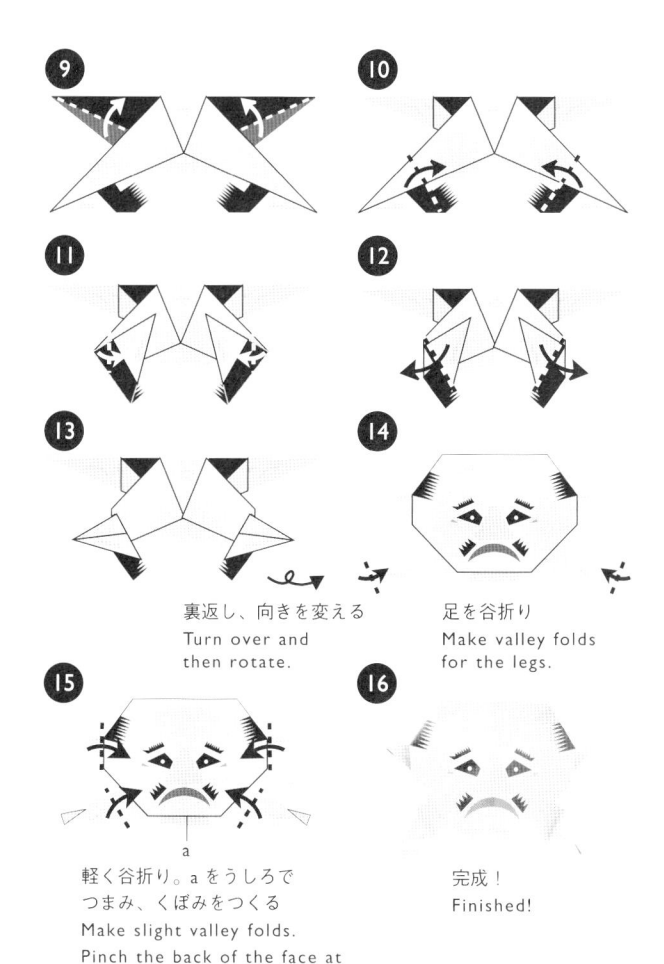

★産女 Ubume → 折り紙 p43

1
2
3
4

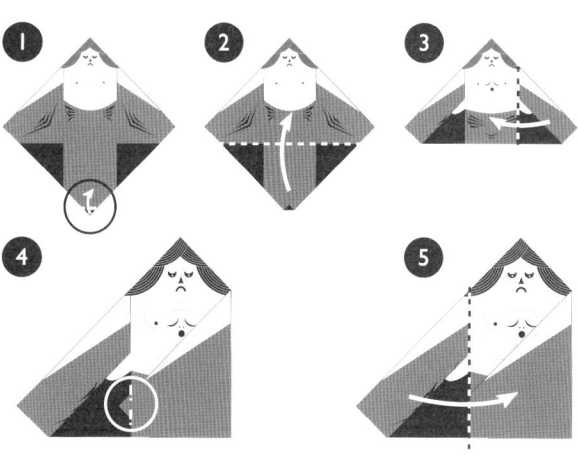

手を軽く山折り
Make a slight mountain fold for the hand.

5
6

手を軽く山折り
Make a slight mountain fold for the hand.

7

手を少し広げる
Open out the arms.

完成！
Finished!

雨降り小僧 Amefuri-Kozō → 折り紙 p47

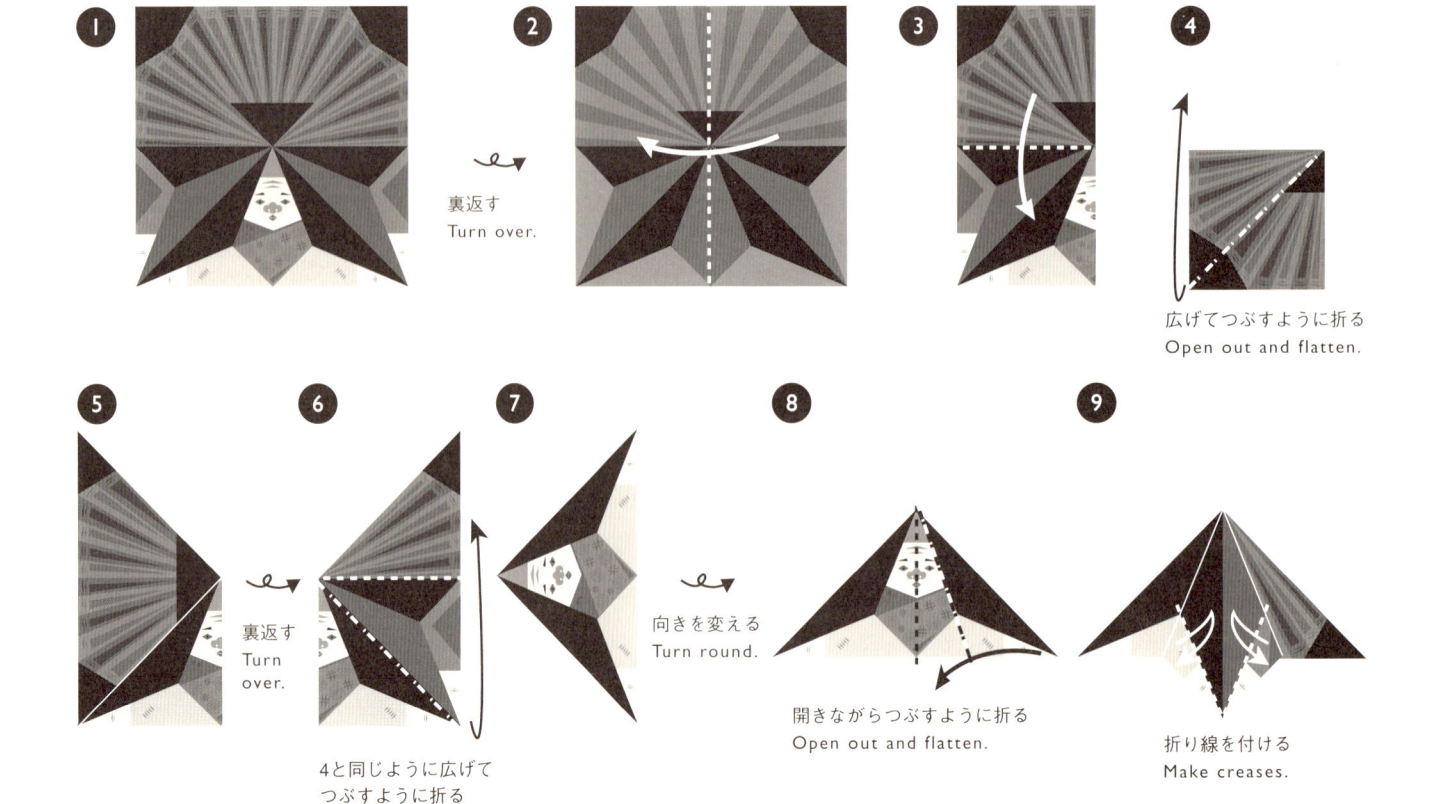

①

② 裏返す Turn over.

③

④ 広げてつぶすように折る Open out and flatten.

⑤ 裏返す Turn over.

⑥ 4と同じように広げてつぶすように折る Do the same to the back.

⑦ 向きを変える Turn round.

⑧ 開きながらつぶすように折る Open out and flatten.

⑨ 折り線を付ける Make creases.

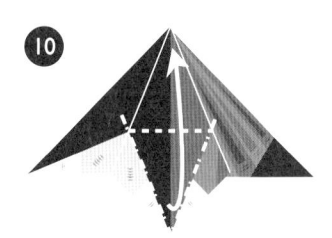

10
折り線を使って内側を広げて
つぶすように折る
Open out and flatten along the creases.

11
1枚のみ下に折る
Fold the front flap down.

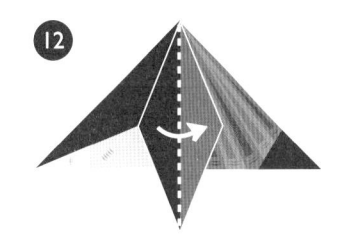

12

13
○側も8,9,10,11,12と同じように折る
Repeat steps 8 to 12 for the side marked by the circle.

14
中割り折りで足を作る
Make an inside reverse fold for the feet.

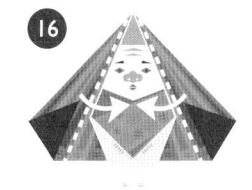

15

16

17
谷折り
Make a valley fold.

18
もう一度谷折り
Make a valley fold.

19
傘を少し開いて
Open out the umbrella.

20
完成!
Finished!

垢嘗め Aka-Name → 折り紙 p49

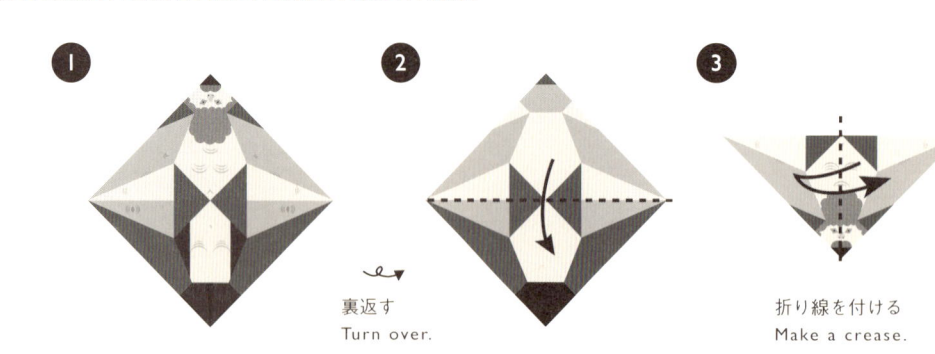

1

2 裏返す Turn over.

3 折り線を付ける Make a crease.

4 折り線を使って○と○を合わせるように開きながらつぶす Open out along the crease and then fold over so the two circles meet.

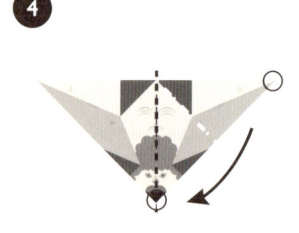

5 a側も4と同じように折る Do the same to the back.

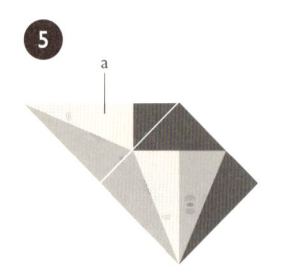

6 折り線を付ける Make creases.

7 折り線を使って内側を広げてつぶすように折る Open out and flatten along the creases.

8 裏返す Turn over.

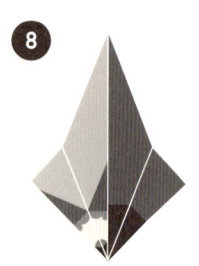

9 折り線を付ける Make creases.

84

10 折り線を使って内側を広げてつぶすように折る
Open out and flatten along the creases.

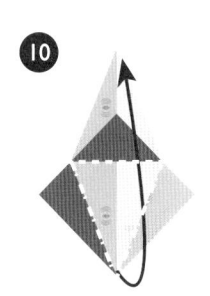

11 上の1枚のみ内側に折る
Fold the front flap on the dotted line.

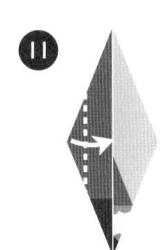

12

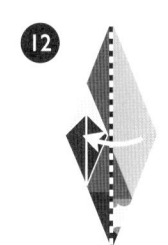

13  裏返し、向きを変える
Turn over, and upside down.

14

15

16 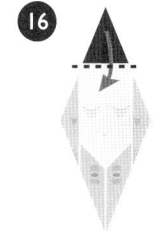 1枚のみ下におろす
Fold the front flap down.

17 1枚のみ下におろす
Fold the front flap down.

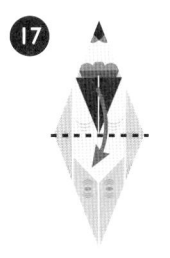

18 広げてつぶすように折り、顔を出す
Open out and flatten.

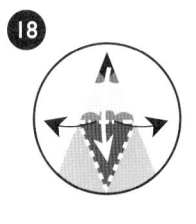

19 内側へ山折り
Fold back using a mountain fold.

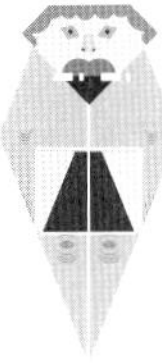

20 aを顔の中に入れる
Place in the mouth.

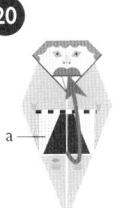

21 中割り折りで足を作る
Make an inside reverse fold for the feet.

22 舌を段々になるように折る
Make stair fold on the tongue.

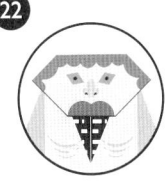

23 完成！
Finished!

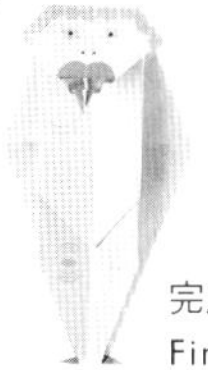

網切り Ami-Kiri → 折り紙 p51

1

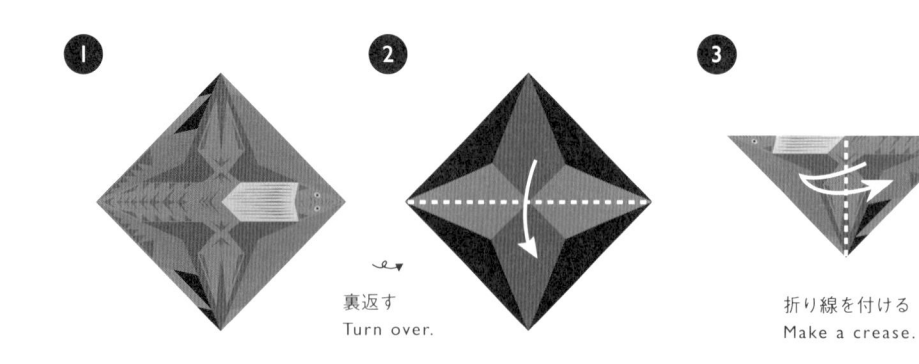

2 裏返す
Turn over.

3 折り線を付ける
Make a crease.

4 折り線を使って○と○を合わせるように開きながらつぶす
Open out along the crease and then fold over so the two circles meet.

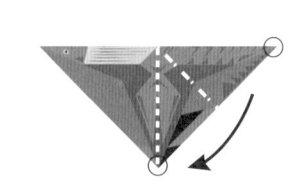

5 a側も4と同じように折る
Do the same to the back.

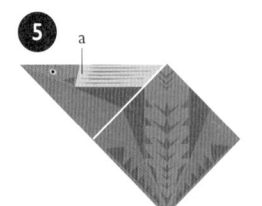

6 折り線を付ける
Make creases.

7 折り線を使って内側を広げてつぶすように折る
Open out and flatten along the creases.

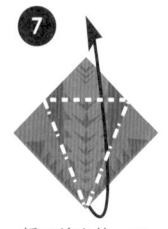

8 裏返す
Turn over.

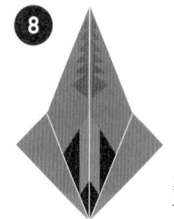

9 折り線を付ける
Make creases.

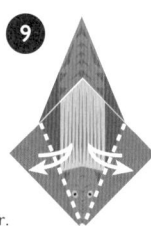

10 折り線を使って内側を広げてつぶすように折る
Open out and flatten along the creases.

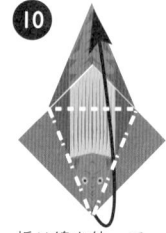

11 1枚のみ谷折り
Fold the front flap down.

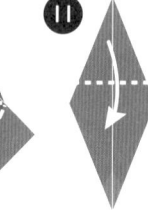

12
裏返す
Turn over.

13
2枚重ねて谷折り
Fold both flaps together using valley folds.

14

15

16
裏返し、向きを変える
Turn over, and upside down.

17
軽く山折り
Make a slight mountain fold.

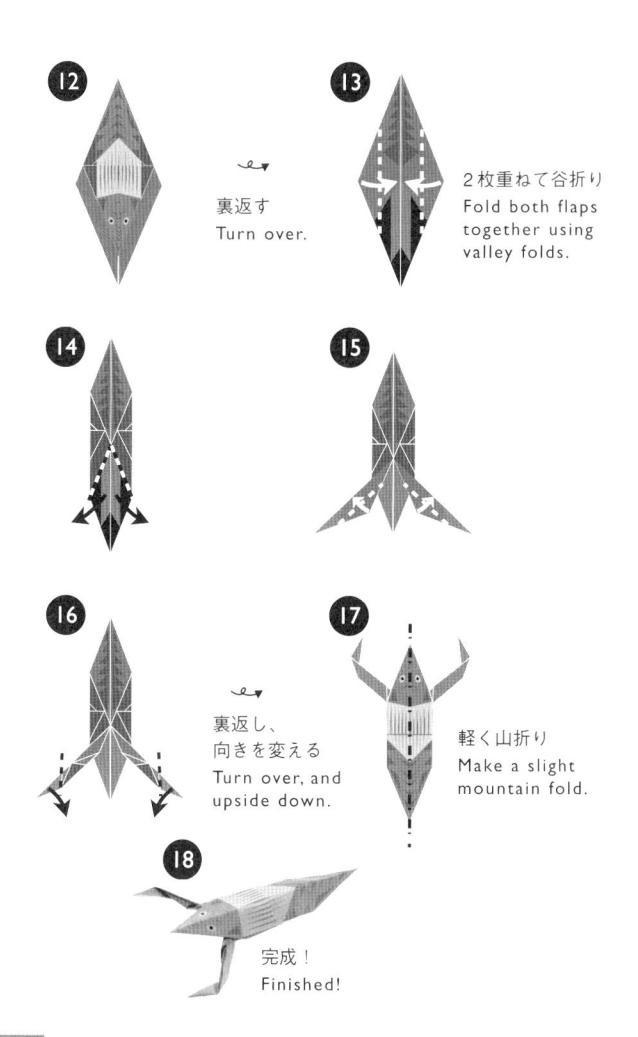

18
完成！
Finished!

87

★★ ぬれ女 Nure-Onna → 折り紙 p53

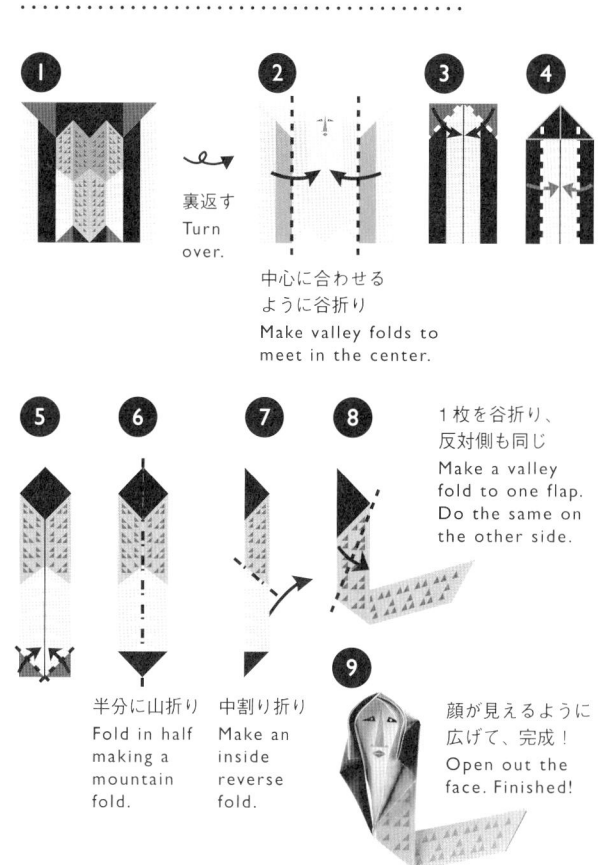

1
裏返す
Turn over.

2
中心に合わせるように谷折り
Make valley folds to meet in the center.

3

4

5
半分に山折り
Fold in half making a mountain fold.

6

7
中割り折り
Make an inside reverse fold.

8
1枚を谷折り、反対側も同じ
Make a valley fold to one flap. Do the same on the other side.

9
顔が見えるように広げて、完成！
Open out the face. Finished!

★★★
二本足 Nihon-Ashi → 折り紙 p55

1. 裏返す
Turn over.

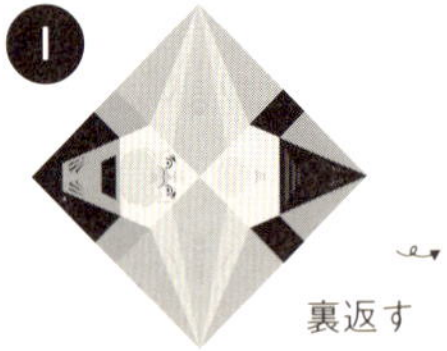

2.

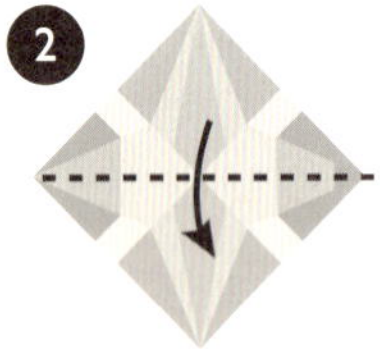

3.  折り線を付ける
Make a crease.

4. 折り線を使って○と○を合わせるように開きながらつぶす
Open out along the crease and then fold over so the two circles meet.

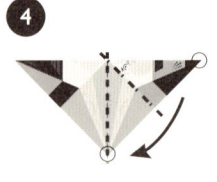

5. 裏側も4と同じように折る
Do the same to the back.

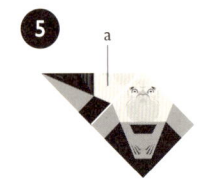

6.

7.  折り線を使って内側を広げてつぶすように折る
Open out and flatten along the creases.

8.

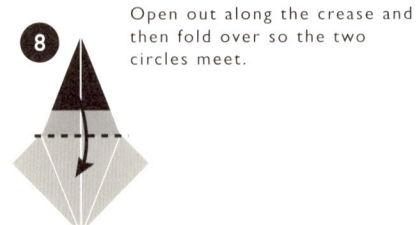

9.

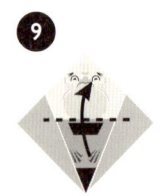

10.  裏返す
Turn over.

11. 折り線を付ける
Make creases.

12. 折り線を使って内側を広げてつぶすように折る
Open out and flatten along the creases.

13

14

15 1枚めくって違う面を出し、裏面も同様に
Turn over a flap to expose a new side. Do the same to the back.

16

17 裏返す
Turn over.

折ったところ
The shape after step 16.

18

19 折ったところ
The shape after step 18.

20 1枚めくって違う面を出し、裏面も同様に
Turn over a flap. Do the same to the back.

21 根元から中割り折り
Make inside reverse folds from the base.

22 中割り折りをくり返して足を作る
Make more inside reverse folds for the feet.

23

24 内側へ入れる
Tuck in.

25 裏返す
Turn over.

26 内側へ入れる
Tuck in.

裏返す
Turn over.

27 完成！
Finished!

★★★ ろくろ首 Rokuro-Kubi → 折り紙 p57

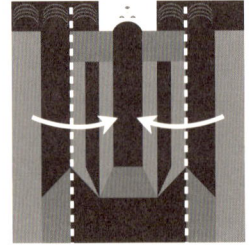

1

2 裏返す
Turn over.

3 中心に合わせるように谷折り
Make valley folds to meet in the center.

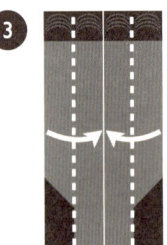

4 山折り
Mountain fold.

5

6 折り線を付ける
Make a crease.

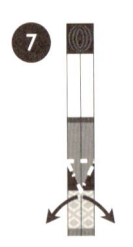

7 折り線を使って首を立てながら広げる
Open out either side of the crease to make the neck.

8 折ったところ
The shape after step 7.

9 1枚だけ○の部分をつまんで開く
Pinching the circles, pull up and open out.

10 開いた状態
The shape after step 9.

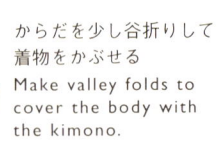

11 裏返す
Turn over.

からだを少し谷折りして着物をかぶせる
Make valley folds to cover the body with the kimono.

12 髪を開かせる
Pull out for the hair.

13 首を細くする
Make the neck thin.

14 首を曲げる
Twist the neck.

15 完成！
Finished!

★★★ 小豆洗い Azuki-Arai → 折り紙 p59

①

② 裏返す
Turn over.

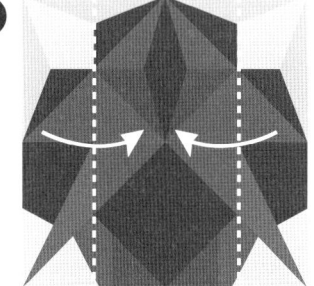

③ 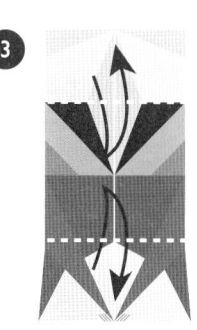 折り線を付ける
Make creases.

④ 広げてつぶすように折る
Open out and flatten.

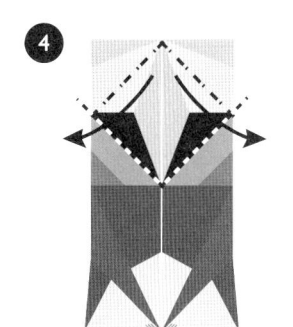

⑤ 広げてつぶすように折る
Open out and flatten.

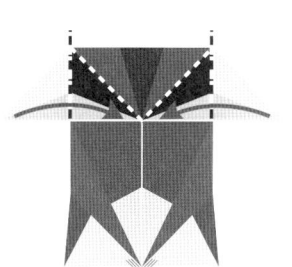

⑥ 内側を広げて
つぶすように折る
Pull out the inside
and flatten.

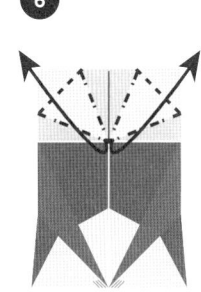

⑦

⑧ 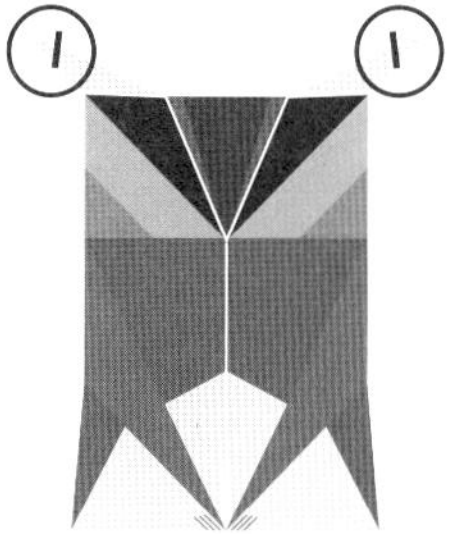 中割り折りで足を作る
Make an inside
reverse fold for the
feet.

91

9
折り線を使って内側を
広げてつぶすように折る
Open out and flatten
along the creases.

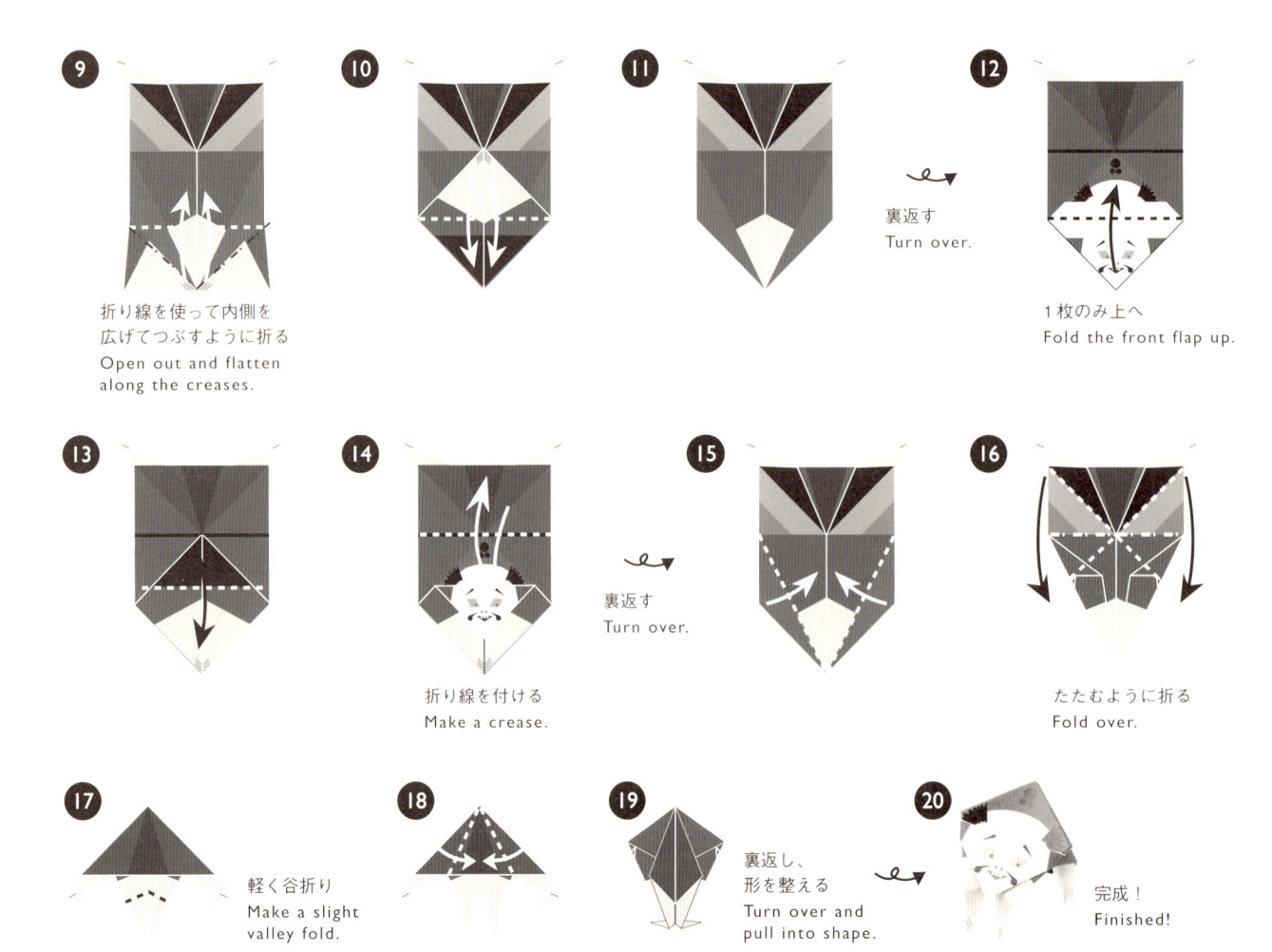

10

11
裏返す
Turn over.

12
1枚のみ上へ
Fold the front flap up.

13

14
折り線を付ける
Make a crease.

15
裏返す
Turn over.

16
たたむように折る
Fold over.

17
軽く谷折り
Make a slight
valley fold.

18

19
裏返し、
形を整える
Turn over and
pull into shape.

20
完成
Finished!

92

★★★ 河童 Kappa → 折り紙 p61

1.

2. 裏返す
Turn over.

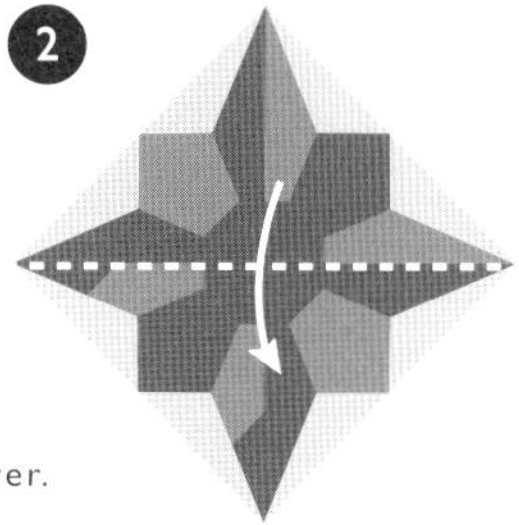

3. 折り線を付ける
Make a crease.

4. 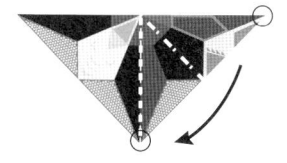 折り線を使って○と○を合わせるように開きながらつぶす
Open out along the crease and then fold over so the two circles meet.

5. a側も4と同じように折る
Do the same to the back.

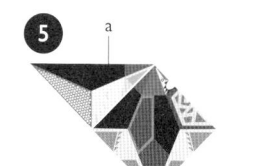

6. 開きながらつぶす
Open out and flatten.

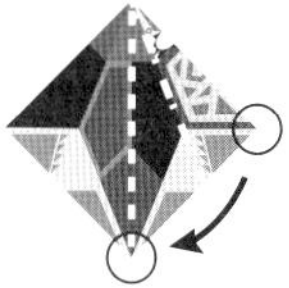

7. 開きながらつぶす
Open out and flatten.

8. 残りの全ての面を6,7と同じように折る
Do the same to all surfaces.

9.

10.  1枚めくって違う面を出す
Turn over a flap.

11.

12.  中割り折りで手を作りながら1枚めくる
Make an inside reverse fold to a flap for the arm.

13. ○側も10,11,12と同じように折る
Do the same on the side marked with a circle.

93

⑭

⑮
裏返す
Turn over.

⑯
中割り折りで
足を作る
Make an inside
reverse fold for
the feet.

⑰

⑱

⑲
座らせる
Fold into a
sitting position.

完成！
Finished!

★★ 天井下り　Tenjō-Kudari → 折り紙 p63

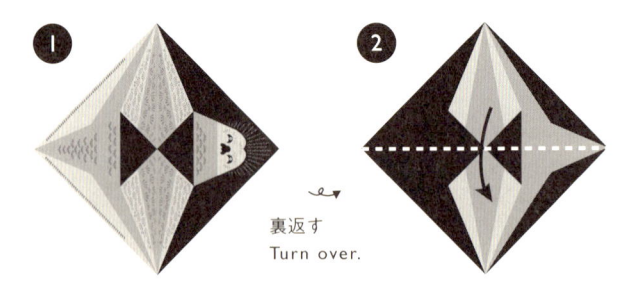

①

②
裏返す
Turn over.

③
折り線を付ける
Make a crease.

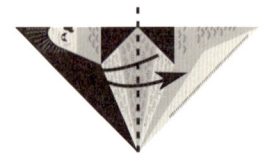

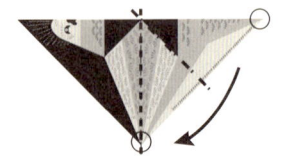

④
折り線を使って○と○を合わ
せるように開きながらつぶす
Open out along the crease
and then fold over so the
two circles meet.

94

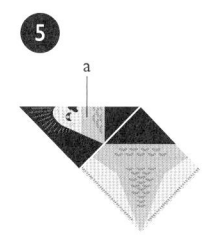

5 a側も4と同じように折る
Do the same to the back.

6 折り線を付ける
Make creases.

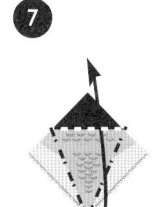

7 折り線を使って内側を広げてつぶすように折る
Open out and flatten along the creases.

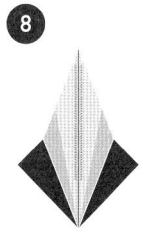

8 裏側も6,7と同じように折る
Do the same to the back.

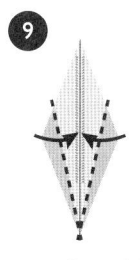

9 上の1枚のみ谷折り
Fold the front flap on dotted line.

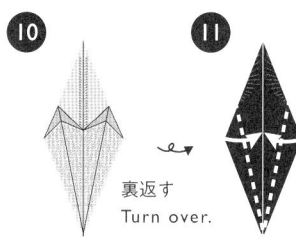

10 裏返す
Turn over.

11 折ったところ
The shape after step 9.

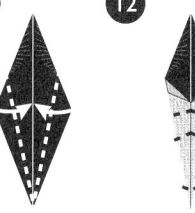

12 中割り折りをくり返し手を作る
Make several inside reverse folds for the arms.

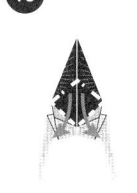

13 折り線を使って開きながらつぶすように折る
Open out and flatten along the creases.

14 向きを変える
Turn round.

15 後ろへ折る
Fold back.

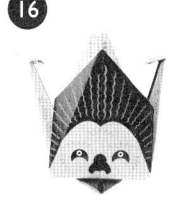

16 完成！
Finished!

cochae（こちゃえ）

軸原ヨウスケと武田美貴を中心にした紙遊びのグラフィック・ユニット。「紙遊びをPOPに！」をテーマに、グラフィック折り紙、紙のパズル、新しい視点をもった玩具の作製等、幅広い活動を行っている。本作には、旧メンバーの光森康郎も参加。著書に『折りCA』（青幻舎）、『ぬりえおりがみ』（ビジネス社）。オリガミキットやオリガミてぬぐいなどを自主制作している。本書の続編として『めでた尽くし』も好評発売中。

Cochae is the dynamic graphic arts unit run by Yosuke Jikuhara and Miki Takeda whose main aim is to popularize "fun with paper" through such innovative games as art origami and paper puzzles. They produced this book in collaboration with their former partner Yasuo Mitsumori. Their publications include *Ori-CA* and *Nurie Origami*. They have also created an origami kit and origami towel.

図版協力　川崎市市民ミュージアム、
　　　　　東北大学附属図書館、松井文庫
主な参考文献　『妖怪事典』（毎日新聞社）
　　　　　『図説日本妖怪大全』（講談社＋α文庫）
　　　　　『図説日本妖怪大鑑』（講談社＋α文庫）
　　　　　『図説日本の妖怪』（河出書房新社）
　　　　　『妖怪談義』（講談社学術文庫）
　　　　　『にっぽん妖怪地図』（角川書店）

おとなのORIGAMI-BOOK　cochaeのグラフィック折り紙

妖怪おりがみ

発行日　2008年4月18日　第1刷
　　　　2018年4月18日　第10刷
著　者　cochae
発行者　渡瀬昌彦
発行所　株式会社講談社
　　　　〒112-8001 東京都文京区音羽2-12-21
　　　　電話　編集　03-5395-3529
　　　　　　　販売　03-5395-3606
　　　　　　　業務　03-5395-3615
印刷所　NISSHA株式会社
製本所　大口製本印刷株式会社

©cochae 2008, Printed in Japan

定価はカバーに表示してあります。
落丁本・乱丁本は購入書店名を明記のうえ、小社業務宛にお送り下さい。
送料小社負担にてお取り替えします。なお、この本についてのお問い合わせは、生活文化宛にお願いいたします。
本書のコピー、スキャン、デジタル化等の無断複製は著作権法上での例外を除き禁じられています。本書を代行業者等の第三者に依頼してスキャンやデジタル化することはたとえ個人や家庭内の利用でも著作権法違反です。

ISBN978-4-06-261762-8　N.D.C. 790　96p　15cm

編集協力／町田陽子
アートディレクション／坂川栄治
デザイン／田中久子、永井亜矢子
英訳／Ginny Tapley
英文校正／Haruko Horiuchi
撮影／講談社写真部（渡辺充俊）